AUTHOR	Kane McLaughlin
TITLE	Justin Webb Notes on them & us

DATE DUE	BORROWER'S NAME
11	

NOTES

ON THE M

AND

US

JUSTIN WEBB

First published in 2011 by

Short Books
3A Exmouth House
Pine Street
EC1R 0JH

10 9 8 7 6 5 4 3 2 1

A CIP catalogue record for this book is available from the British Library.

ISBN 978-1-907595-43-1

Printed and bound by CPI Group (UK) Ltd, Croydon, CR0 4YY

Cover design: Nathan Burton

To Sarah, Sam, Martha and Clara

Contents

Chapter One

"Relax,"said the Night Man.
"We are programmed to receive.
You can check out any time you like,
but you can never leave…"
The Eagles, "Hotel California"

AMERICA WAS NOT designed to be left. The opposite, in fact – it was designed to be arrived in. It was programmed to receive and – as was the case in The Eagles' song – there is some wonderment at the front desk when you try to go.

When our time came to leave after eight years of living in the US, we approached the checkout with typical Englishness. For effect, we exaggerated our sadness at the end of our time in America. The result? Confusion.

"Our British home is in south London so we'll probably all be murdered before Christmas," we said to friends.

"Oh, my gosh. Um, why not stay?" they replied, anxiously.

Because you have no sense of humour, would be one answer. But that (while being partly true) is not fair. Like so many other misunderstimations of them by us and us by them, it hangs there, unchallenged, in the ether. In eight years of life in America, I came to value – to love, actually – the stolid, sunny, unchallenging, simple virtuousness of the American suburban psyche. But back in England, as well as being reintroduced to the darkness, to the can't-do spirit, to what I saw from afar as the drunken directionlessness of British national life, I have seen a side to Britain that I had (to my shame) rather forgotten existed. It's a richness born of knowing, rather than hoping. Contentedness rather than striving. And, yes, humour.

The woman who was to sell our house in Washington was a prime specimen of Americana. She was hellishly perky. Nothing got her down, not even the fact that we were selling in the midst of the biggest depression since the Great Flood. In this area it was different.

"You have a lovely home!"

But she thought we had too many books. She did not say so but she talked of creating spaces on the shelves – for snow-globes, perhaps, or silver photo frames filled with perfect children showing off perfect teeth.

This is a cultural thing. When selling a home in America, you have to pretend that you do not live there. In fact, you have to pretend that no one lives there. Or ever has. Previously owned homes are of course the norm for us Europeans. We understand that other generations have made their mark, lived their lives and passed on to the great home in the sky. This means – as we English know, having grown up with rattling windows and mouldy grouting and those ghosts of the past – that no home will be perfect. They do not make such allowances in America.

So the inspector's report into our Washington house, the survey, was the cause of much delibera- tion and soul-searching from our potential buyers. An outside light was not working properly. A tap was leaking. A chimney needed investigation. As I read it, my mind turned to our house in London which is actually falling down – somebody omitted to prop up the middle when an arch was cut in a downstairs room 100 years ago – but which is still eminently saleable. The English understand that *we are all falling down.*

Dust to dust, we intuit. Americans do not. They have not got there yet.

In the months before we left the US, I paid the highest tribute to my sense of Americanness: I visited a full body scanning clinic whose CT x-ray scans were advertised on local radio. These scans are part and parcel of American middle-class life. They use high-powered technology that in Britain is the preserve of hospitals and truly ill people. In America you can simply go to your local mall, pay a hefty fee and, in theory, leave armed with a set of scans that tell you precisely how your body is ticking along. The company motto might well epitomise the attitude to life of the whole nation: "Now you have the power to see your future and change it." The phrase is the copyright possession of Virtual Physical of Rockville, Maryland, so if you are a GP about to take control of your own budgets in Cleethorpes, do not on any account use it. Ah, but of course you wouldn't. Not in a million years. You wouldn't make that claim, and no Brit would believe you if you did.

Truth be told, while I lived there I decided I would rather be them than us. I admired the concern over the chimney and the belief that any problem (even those associated with my fast-declining body) could be fixed. Before I left, I sat one evening on the porch, in the growing heat of the Washington spring, listening to the cicadas chirruping and the sound of lawns being mowed, and yearned to be staying. It would be so easy, so uncomplicated, so safe. One phrase in particular from the folder I took home from Virtual Physical in Rockville caught my imagination: "Examination of the brain reveals no definite abnormalities!" Had it been otherwise, were it to be otherwise in the future, the implication is that these abnormalities would be zapped faster that you could say "Take me home to my white picket fences". How comforting. And yet of course this comfort– like the perfect home we tried to create – is, to put it mildly, an illusion.

From Washington, let me take you south by 600 miles or so to the state of South Carolina and to the city of Charleston, where the American South begins. In the summer of 2007, I drove Route 17 south in the steamy heat, with the breeze all but non-existent, out of Charleston and down into the low country, the salt marshes. Charleston is one of America's most elegant cities, but Route 17 is not on any tourist maps, at least not as an attraction in its own right. In a sense, though, it should be. It gives a wonderful insight into hardscrabble American life, the sleazy glamour of the road that repels and appeals to visitors – and indeed Americans themselves – in roughly equal measure: gas stations, tattoo parlours, Bojangles Pizza, $59-a-night motels, pawn shops, gun shops, car showrooms, nail bars, and Piggly Wiggly, the local supermarket chain which, in my limited experience, smells almost as odd as it sounds. Piggly Wiggly, by the way, was the world's first supermarket. Mr Piggly and Mr Wiggly – I am guessing at the etymology but I may well be right – had the then revolutionary idea of abolishing the high counter that, in shops of yesteryear, came between the shopper and the goods. It was a move that has affected the world as much as the invention of the light bulb or the washing machine, but Piggly Wiggly just don't seem too darn fussed. That's life in the South. That's life on Route 17 – stolid and ragged and smelling slightly of petrol and chicken fried in motor oil.

It is a panorama of the mundane: Doric columns a-plenty but all of them made of cheap concrete and attached to restaurants or two-bit accountants' offices. On and on it goes, encroaching into the palm forests with no hint of apology.

The following morning I found myself standing next to a black four-wheel-drive vehicle and another quintessentially American phenomenon: a politician mired in Bible-laced hypocrisy.

At the time I met Mark Sanford, the then Governor of South Carolina whom I had made the journey to

Charleston to meet and profile for the BBC, I didn't know about the hypocrisy. But I should have guessed when he offered to let me in on a secret. He was a closet tiller of fields, he said, and liked nothing better than to get out with his boys and work the land. He took me for a drive in his Governor's limo and after a few minutes we slowed and took a turn down a lane that ended in a field. It was hot. Under a tree stood the Governor's tractor. The limo was parked, the clothes changed, and (like Gladstone with his tree felling) the Governor began ploughing. Up and down, up and down, through the heat haze. It was a wholesome picture that we duly shot for our profile.

In fact, it was a little too wholesome to be true. Weeks after telling me that all-American story, it emerged that Sanford was also ploughing furrows in foreign fields. The Governor disappeared for a few days, and was eventually tracked down to Buenos Aires, where he was found with an Argentine woman who was not Mrs Sanford, and with whom it transpired that he had been having a lengthy affair. This behaviour from a man so Christian and God-fearing that, when he was a congressman, he lived in some peculiar Christian fellowship house in DC. It did not stop his Doric columns from being false. He lost his job and with it the chance of vying to be the Republican presidential candidate in 2012. He was eaten alive by a public, half of whom were probably jealous of his Argentine adventure but all of whom no doubt attended those mean little churches that dot South Carolina, the signs outside them saying things like "Don't make me have to come down and sort you out: God!"

And yet for all the ugliness, the deadening tawdriness of much of the American landscape and the tinny feebleness of many of its politicians – the Tea Party Senate candidate who was once a witch, the former Democratic Governor of Illinois who tried to sell Barack Obama's old Senate seat and now advertises pistachio nuts for a living – for all that nastiness and shallowness and flakiness, there is no question in my mind that to live there was the greatest privilege of my life. And we still have much to learn from the way our cousins have ploughed their furrows, with the mental equipment they took over to the New World. We can benefit from seeing ourselves now, in the modern age, through their eyes. And they can benefit from returning the compliment.

Our relationship with America – not Mr Cameron's relationship with Mr Obama, but truly *all of our* relationships with *all of them*; our understanding of their way of life and their grasp of ours – is important for two reasons. First, it is the cornerstone of the English-speaking world, which has so dominated the history of the globe in recent centuries and contributed enormously to the health, wealth and happiness of everyone. To accept this, you do not have to subscribe to the view that everything that the English-speaking world has done has been glorious and right, or that non-English-speaking peoples have contributed little to human progress; but the thrust of recent history has been provided by the people who brought you Magna Carta, the Glorious Revolution, the Declaration of Independence and the openness to innovation and democratisation that encouraged the greatest accumulation of wealth the world has ever seen. To an extent that torch was passed to the West with the *Mayflower*, but not entirely. Americans can still learn from Britain and still do. And we from them – not least, as *The Times* remarked in a wistful editorial after Barack Obama's visit to London in May 2011, in the area of self-confidence and assertiveness: we have lost our ability to trumpet our achievements and recognise our worth; they have not.

Secondly, America belongs to us as much as to them. The immensity of America, its energy and zest for life, used to remind me sometimes of India. And like India, where I spent some time for the BBC many moons ago, America shines a light on the entire human condition. Few other nations really do. Italy reveals truths about Italians, Afghanistan about Afghans, Fiji about Fijians. But America speaks to the whole of humanity because the whole of humanity is represented there; our possibilities and our propensities. Often what is revealed is unpleasant; truths that are not attractive or wholesome or hopeful. On the last day we spent in our home in north-west Washington, a burger bar at the end of our street was holding an eating competition. The sight was nauseating: acne-ridden youths, several already obese, stuffing meat and buns into their mouths while local television reporters, the women in dinky pastel suits, rushed around getting the best shots. America can be seen as little more than an eating competition: a giant, gaudy, manic effort to stuff grease and gunge into already-sated innards. You could argue that the sub-prime mortgage crisis – the Ground Zero of the great recession and arguably an event or set of events more damaging than 9/11 – was caused mainly by greed: a lack of proportion, a lack of proper respect for the natural way of things that persuaded companies to stuff mortgages into the mouths of folks whose credit rating was always likely to induce an eventual spray of vomit.

There is an intellectual ugliness as well: a dark age lurking; a book-burning tendency never far from the surface of American life, even when the President has been to Harvard. For me this darkness was epitomised by the death in Wisconsin of a little girl who should still be alive. Eleven-year-old Kara Neumann was suffering from Type One diabetes, an autoimmune condition my son Sam also has. Her family, for religious reasons, decided not to take her to hospital when she fell ill. Instead, they prayed by her bedside and she died.

The night before she died – and she would have been in intense discomfort – her parents called the founder of a religious website and prayed with him over the telephone. But they did not call a doctor.

If Kara had been taken to hospital, even at that late stage, insulin could have saved her. She could have been home in a few days and chirpy by the end of the week, as my son was in the same situation. It was an entirely preventable death caused, let's be frank, by some of the Stone Age superstition that stalks the richest and most technologically advanced nation on earth. I deplore the superstition and the eating competitions and the tatty dreariness of so much of this country, but I am convinced that these aspects of America are not the flip side of its greatness, as some believe, but actually part of that greatness. You cannot have the good without the bad: there is something about the carelessness of America that gives space for greatness.

Out on Route 17 in South Carolina, you can do very well or very badly. You can crash and burn, or you can fill up with cheap petrol and ride on into the sunset. If you do not like yourself in South Carolina, you can hire a self-drive truck and take it to Seattle. If you do not like your life and you have ambition and a little luck, you can change it because – being American – you believe you can change it.

Sitting in a dingy New York apartment watching Perry Mason on the TV, you can decide to make it big in law as eight-year-old Sonia Sotomayor, also suffering from Type One diabetes, once did. In 2009, by now in her fifties and having triumphed over poverty and daily insulin injections and the health scares that will have accompanied her condition, she was a Supreme Court Justice and the latest American story to send shivers down the spines of dreamers of the American dream.

But if Sonia Sotomayor can make it big, there must be something creating the drive, and part of that something is the poverty of the alternative, the discomfort of the ordinary lives that most Americans endure and the freedom that Americans have to go to hell if they want to. This is the atmosphere in which Nobel

Prize-winners are nurtured. A nation that will one day mass-produce a cure for Type One diabetes could not – would not – save little Kara Neumann from the bovine idiocy of her religious parents. More than 310 million people live in America now, settlers from all over the world. From Ho Chi Minh City, from Timbuktu, from Vilnius, from Tehran, from every last corner of the earth; they have made America their home and they are still streaming in.

And yet there is something missing. And that, to an extent, is where we come in. America has lost sight, I think, of some of the subtleties of human life, some of the political compromises and mental accommodations that go towards making the good life on earth and are arguably part of the reason that English-speaking peoples have been as successful as they have. America is future-focused to be sure, and in many ways benefits from this attitude; but the place has become crazed by fights over fundamental world-views that actually do not matter very much. The Obama presidency has coincided with, and to some extent caused, a fight to the death over culture that America really does not need to have. In the Britain of the coalition government we have battles about the here and now: the future is for folks to whom we have not been introduced and about whom we do not currently care.

We still get drunk together, while sober Americans seethe and plot.

Having said that, this book is anything but a serious political text. It is intended as a snapshot of a rather odd moment in history, where the go-getters got their knickers in a twist, while the old country plodded on. A moment when the highly respected and serious-minded American political commentator David Brooks made a journey to Britain and found that, for the first time ever, he had left a pessimistic place and come east to a more optimistic one. Britain is phlegmatic and practical in the modern age; America is behaving like a middle-aged man in the grip of a full-scale mid-life crisis. America has gone out and bought a motorbike and is driving it too fast. Mr and Mrs America argue constantly – she thinks he is mad and he thinks she is dull and ugly. Our cousins are in a mess. Even the killing of Osama bin Laden – an event of seismic political importance in the US, utterly underestimated in most British reporting – failed to do the trick. That provides an opportunity for Britons who like and admire America to rethink the relationship we should have with it in the future; to rethink the reality of both the ties that bind us and the utter separateness of some of our customs and heritage. So this is about them and us and, most importantly, the space between which is filled sometimes with distrust and venom and sometimes with genuine communion of spirit.

It is about the special relationship. There: I have said it. The latest twist is that the relationship has become essential rather than special. And the White House now understands that while special was silly, essential is, well, essential. I doubt it. On my last day at the White House I was thrown out of the study of a senior official when I mentioned the special relationship. "Gettoutahere!" he screamed. "You people are all mad." Obama folks felt, and feel, that they have more important things to focus on. They are right, probably, but that need not stop us thinking about these matters and coming up with a vision of them and us that genuinely accords with history and fits the times.

Chapter Two

Special relationship… oh that's all bollocks!
Former foreign secretary in conversation with
the author, 2011

Ours is not just a special relationship,
it is an essential relationship – for us and for the world.
Barack Obama and David Cameron, May 2011

ONE OF THE first acts of the Obama administration –
before they tackled the economic crisis and reformed
their health system, long before they began the effort
to come to grips with Afghanistan, or engaged with
Russia, or tried and failed to close Guantanamo, or
shot Osama bin Laden – was the removal of a bust of
Sir Winston Churchill from the Oval Office.

It was reported at the time that they chucked poor
Winston in a taxi and sent him home to the British

embassy. It appeared to be an act of gross callousness, particularly given the fact that most Washington taxis are driven by cheerful Ethiopians with little knowledge of the streets outside central Addis Ababa. Winston might have ended up in some flop-house in crime-ridden Southeast DC, a doorstop for a drug dealer's moll, or worse. The news was broken by the ever-energetic and well-connected Tom Baldwin then of the *Times*, a traditionalist with a sense of history first encouraged, no doubt, by his tutors at Balliol College, Oxford. But Tom's story was followed up by less well-educated and more excitable British newspaper reporters who reached for predictable tropes when they found out: *Britain snubbed by the new President! The special relationship itself sent packing in a cab!* There was even a motive found: Churchill's crackdown on the Mau Mau rebels in Kenya had led to the imprisonment of Obama's paternal grandfather. *It was revenge!* In spite of the fact that Obama's relationship with his father was (famously) distant and with his grandfather genuinely non-existent, nothing got in the way of the narrative that this was a snub delivered to an old ally.

Months later I was in the White House talking to a person I have to call a "senior administration official", though I can tell you that if you follow

American politics, you will have heard of this chap. "Why did you do it?" I asked.

"You folks are obsessed," was his reply. "We were just clearing house. We didn't even know who it was... we thought it was Eisenhower: elderly white folks all look alike to us."

He was only half joking.

It is not that the Obama administration had any particular dislike for Britain and the British. Exacting revenge for the wrongs done to the Mau Mau was way down their to-do list, frankly somewhere near the bottom. It had never been mentioned on the campaign trail (how delicious if it had been: "Ohio, I make this pledge to you, we are Americans and as Americans we know that the Mau Mau's values are our values"). But what the British press picked up, what they sensed right from the start, what caused them to be prickly and dyspeptic, was that the focus of this President was not on us and never would be. Americans thought we might have noticed this by now. To sophisticated East Coast commentators, the demise of Britain – *lost an empire and not yet found a role* – is nothing new to report; a *Newsweek* article about the Churchill flap raised its journalistic eyebrow and enquired, laconically: "Has America's even-tempered new President already ruffled feathers in the land that spawned Borat and Benny Hill?"

And Churchill! our papers screamed. *We spawned him as well! Quite recently!* But most of America was having none of it, and in those heady days before the Obama presidency fell from grace, most Americans backed him, if they even noticed the row at all.

So just to make the point, we had another. Gordon Brown came to Washington and to the White House and was treated with what the hyperventilating British press (even those who regarded Brown as a villain) saw as grotesque discourtesy. Amid a list of complaints that was, as one American paper sniffed, "longer than Magna Carta", was that the Browns gave the President a rather fancy gift and received utter tat in return. The facts suggest... well, that it was true. The Brown gift was a pen-holder crafted from the timbers of the nineteenth century British anti-slaving warship HMS *President* (whose sister ship, HMS *Resolute*, provided the wood for the Oval Office's desk). Not bad. Thoughtful. Tasteful. *Au point.* The Obama gift was – as you doubt-less remember because it was the moment you began to think that Obama was less than a full saint – 25 DVDs of American movies. *He's Just Not That Into You* was not one of them, but reading between the lines that was the message. Less reported at the time but equally careless: the gifts for the Brown children were models of Marine One, the presidential helicopter. You can get these anywhere, including the White House gift shop, which is where they probably came from. The whole visit was a mess, a *train wreck,* to use the wonderful American expression. Didn't Obama care? Didn't he *know* about *us?* Hadn't someone warned the new President that everything hinged on America's relationship with the Brits?

Evidently not. And here is why not: because it does not. Whether it is special or whether it is essential, it is, like the Monty Python parrot, an ex-relationship. Fine words in Westminster Hall do not change that fact.

The lofty view first: when you place the so-called special relationship alongside the relationship the USA has with China, with Russia, with the EU, with Israel and the Palestinians, with Iran, with Iraq, with Pakistan, with India, with emerging nations such as Brazil – well, you hear what I am saying: it ain't that special.

David Cameron made much of seeking new partnerships in his foreign policy, and the same goes for the Americans. More than any other recent presidency, the Obama administration needs to make the case to the American people that the world's only superpower must recalibrate its relationship with the rest of the planet. This is partly the result of setbacks America experienced following the hubris and the indebtedness of the Bush years, but partly too it is the result of the rise of the rest of the world, the emergence of China and India and Brazil, the stubborn refusal of Russia to fade into memory. Drinking Scotch with British prime ministers, while fiddling absent-mindedly with the head of Winston Churchill and listening to a tape of Edward Murrow, does not really do it. The Obama administration was rather rude to Gordon Brown. The gifts were not desperately well thought through, but the debacle illustrated an important point. The special relationship does not exist. This President, and any modern American president, must be interested primarily in reaching out to other nations. Henry Kissinger is said to have wanted a number to call when he wanted to speak to Europe: now we have a number (step forward Baroness Ashton, the EU Foreign Minister) but they ain't calling any more except as an occasionally remembered courtesy. Times have changed. I saw Henry Kissinger in London in 2011 and he spoke warmly about the special relationship, but quite what it was, he could not clearly say. It's like a ghost, or an imaginary friend in the airing cupboard. It's private: it is a creature of the mind rather than the real world.

Shortly after President Obama was elected, a frustrated viewer wrote to the BBC. Why, he demanded, had the corporation not thought to send Justin Webb to interview the new man? Was it not recognised that this would be interesting? Were we not aware that this presidency would be consequential and did we not think it worth expending a little energy, a taxi fare at least, in getting the scoop? Ah, if only he knew. We had, in truth, come up with the idea of interviewing Obama ourselves. Indeed, during the campaign I had tried repeatedly to persuade his senior staff that the presidential candidate might care to signal how different he was by granting a sit-down interview to a foreigner. "I hear what you say" was as far as it went. I thought at one stage that I might change their minds by catching a ground-breaking few minutes with the great rival for the Democratic Party nomination, Hillary Clinton. I managed to get face to face with her on a rope-line in New Hampshire and launched into my exclusive chat. She smiled at the man in front of me and the child beside me. She answered a question posed by an elderly woman to my left about her brooch. Then she moved on, unmoved by my second question or my third or fourth or fifth. She blanked me more comprehensively that I have ever been blanked by anyone before. I tried everything (including a John

Sergeantesque "Mrs Clinton, here's the microphone!"),
but all for naught. Special relationship?

What I am saying is that it was quite a big deal when
we finally made it to the library of the White House
and to those two chairs facing each other. To celebrate
(as we waited for him), I moved them closer together,
perhaps in subliminal homage to the special relationship that might see our toes touch where the Japanese
reporter or the Swiss would be kept at a distance. But
alas, the rules were the same. A flunky leapt forward:
"Sir, step away from the chairs!" Apparently, they
are placed by protocol officials and no one, not even
Winston Churchill himself, is allowed to move them.
Even Andrew Marr, who followed me to the White
House in 2011, was not, I was pleased to see, allowed
too close.

The entire experience of interviewing Obama served
to underline the death of the special relationship. The
White House, to their credit, never came close to
vetting what questions I was going to ask, but they
made it clear that their central concern was whether
the interview would be translated and replayed by the
World Service. They had no interest in impressing the
folks in Chipping Sodbury. Let them (try to) watch
DVDs. Obama wanted to use the BBC to speak to the
world. The approach was repeated a year later when

the White House granted the BBC its second interview with the President. It could have gone to my successor in Washington or to Andrew Marr or John Humphrys or Adrian Chiles and Christine Bleakley, who were still on the *One Show* sofa and still on the up. It did not. It went to Bakman Kalbassi of the BBC Persian Service. And my information is that the White House was delighted with the results, a strong interview in which the President was pressed hard to give firm answers, and those answers were delivered directly, via a trustworthy translation, into homes in Iran.

So the fact that the President eventually sat down with Andrew Marr, just before coming to Britain on the "essential relationship" tour should be seen in the context of initial concern with the outside world. Andy's interview will have been used on BBC World and that is where the White House will have wanted it to be used.

Sometimes the British people, and British institutions such as the BBC or the Army, can be of use to American administrations. Often they admire the Brits (certainly true in the case of the Army and to a lesser extent the BBC), but it is never about Britain or about their relationship with Britain. There is always more to it. It is about what Britain can do. It is, to quote the man who received the

DVDs, "a partnership of purpose". We offer the partnership, he might have added, and they offer the purpose.

When the Select Committee on Foreign Affairs declared the special relationship over in their report of 2009, the committee chairman, Mike Gapes, officiated at the funeral. I had given evidence to the committee, so I had an inkling of where they were going, but the words used by Mr Gapes are still worth noting:

> The use of the phrase "the special relationship" in its historical sense, to describe the totality of the ever-evolving UK–US relationship, is potentially misleading, and we recommend that its use should be avoided.
>
> Yes, we have a special relationship with the US, but we must remember that so too do other countries including regional neighbours, strategic allies and partners. British and European politicians have been guilty of over-optimism about the extent of influence they have over the US. We must be realistic and accept that globalisation, structural changes and shifts in geopolitical power will inevitably affect the UK–US relationship.
>
> RIP.

And yet. There is a place where the special relationship – not essential but special – still exists. I have been there. Mr Gapes and his committee, by visiting Washington and Washington alone, have not. There are no direct flights from Britain. You have to change. You have to fly on into that pancake bit in the middle of America where, on a cloudless day, the view stretches towards the horizon. Flat farmland and grids of roads with, it seems from 30,000 feet, no cars. If the Foreign Affairs Commitee had managed to slip away from the embassy dinner and the congressional visit and gone down to Reagan Airport (Washington's domestic hub), they could have boarded a flight to somewhere in Middle America – Boise, Idaho, or Wichita, Kansas, or Normal, Illinois (I think you have to change again for Normal but heck, this isn't a timetable), and there the picture would have been very different. There, to be British (alright, English) really counts.

This is the part of America where Tony Blair's journey never ends. Prime Minister Blair (always *Prime Minister*) and Lady Thatcher have morphed into a composite picture of the plucky dependable Brit. Both are revered, and through their good offices, gentle reader, you can be too. But to assume that the attraction is your muscularity (or Blair's and Thatcher's), or your ability to commit British troops to faraway wars, or your (imagined or otherwise) support or past support for these political giants and their policies, is to make a serious mistake.

They love you for your vowels. Imagine you have now arrived in Boise or Wichita or Normal. You are in need of refreshment and you spot, in the out-of-town mall between the airport and the hotel, a Starbucks. In you go and order a muffin and an iced tea. Pandemoniun ensues. Folks are called in from the back office: "Jolene, come here and listen to this man's beautiful voice!" Large ladies with serious religious views consider throwing away their chances of getting to heaven for a moment of madness with this English stranger. You can see it in their eyes. You are glamour. Like Julia Roberts popping into that bookshop in Notting Hill, you cause hearts to flutter.

"Oh, my gosh!" they murmur, as you place your order for a second time, for the cameras, as it were.

I know this because I have done it. I spent much of my eight years working for the BBC in America shamelessly hamming up my Englishness. If impersonating Hugh Grant in a public place is a crime then I must plead guilty. It opens doors. They love it. They feel they know you and they know that you know the Queen, so when they shake your hand they are shaking hers too. I know it didn't work for BP's Tony Hayward but poor Mr Hayward is the exception that proves the rule.

And, to an extent, this Starbucks relationship matters. It puts us at an advantage, for instance, over the Germans. My former colleague Matt Frei, now sadly relegated to Channel 4 News, is an English-educated polyglot of staggering ability, and could easily have revealed himself to be (as he is) German by birth and nationality. Did he? I don't think so. In Boise he was British. The full monty: Westminster and Oxford.

This, of course, is not the special relationship of which the politicians speak. They hardly notice it. It is not documented. It is certainly not essential. But it is real. It will make a difference to you if you go to Normal. It will not get you out of jail, or have you feted if you're accused of destroying an entire national coastline with your carelessly spilled oil. But it will give you the benefit of the doubt if you scrape the sheriff's car while parking. It will reduce speeding tickets: "Officer, as an Englishman, I offer the profoundest of apologies." Sometimes it will afford you special protection. In Corning, Iowa just before the 2008 caucus, I had illegally parked our large crew car outside a café. It was very, very cold, so I volunteered to stay in the vehicle while a producer went in to get the drinks. Behind me a police cruiser pulled up and the officer got out and approached. Obviously he was going to move me on; I was, after all, committing a crime as serious as any he was likely to come across that day. But no: on hearing my accent, the gentle cop demanded that I go into the café as well and warm up and have a real good stay. He would look after the car. Which is what he did, with his lights flashing, until we were ready to move on. To deny the special relationship, in the light of this behaviour, seems churlish in the extreme. Americans like us. They do. They sometimes find us a bit ungodly and a bit over-complicated (though fixed-term parliaments will help here) but they fundamentally believe that we are on the right side, provided we can keep our snobbiness at bay. This is an important point: if we hector Middle Americans as the *Guardian* famously did just before the 2004 election, encouraging readers to write personal letters to voters in Ohio imploring them not to vote for George W. Bush, our accents will begin to grate. The areas targeted by the *Guardian* swung suspiciously towards the sitting President and away from the course of action, a vote for the Democrat John Kerry, that the *Guardian* readers were advocating. I visited a town where some letters had dropped on doormats and the response was fascinating. They were so pleased to see me that the local paper came and took photos. I had to eat for

England. But the letters with Islington postmarks had caused deep offence; the revolutionary war was rekindled in an instant.

But when we talk nicely, they listen. We have a window seat in the Starbucks of Middle America. We are – they think – comfortably familiar. We are not truly foreign. I sensed that at McCain/Palin rallies in 2008, where although quite a few folks associated the BBC with socialism (Rupert Murdoch's message penetrates the boondocks), most were very friendly. They are not so well disposed to all foreigners in these parts. At a town hall meeting I attended, a woman seized the microphone and praised Senator McCain to the rafters while he beamed and grinned. "Obama is not good for America," she asserted. "Yes, ma'am," McCain chirruped. "Obama is a socialist." "Yes, ma'am." "He's an Ay-rab!"

An Ay-rab? McCain looked panicked. This was barmy talk which he instantly knew would look bad outside this small town. He seized the microphone and delivered an unintentionally revealing rebuke: "Ma'am, Senator Obama is not an Ay-rab: he is a family man…"

Which said it all. We are family men, we Brits. Nobody in Middle America would question it and that gives us standing.

But there is a problem. These Americans who regard us as special, who find our accents mellifluous, are not necessarily in the driving seat in the modern United States. Middle Americans who have been making the running in recent times, Sarah Palin's Tea Party crowd, tend to find us less appealing because of our lack of religious spine and our attachment to train travel and carbon trading. The gentler folk, supporters neither of Palin nor Obama, are rather lost when it comes to political clout.

And outside Middle America, where the real business of the nation is done, where the future lives, in towns like San Antonio, Texas, or Phoenix, Arizona, in the Starbucks here your accent, amigo, counts for little. The problem for the special relationship based on what you might call the *Mayflower* Memory Syndrome is that the *Mayflower* rememberers are not in the driving seat in their nation. Obama's America – black, Hispanic, mixed-race America, future America – does not give a button for Olde England. It is coming up to 400 years since the *Mayflower* sailed to the New World. Memories have dimmed. A teenager with a Croatian immigrant mother and a Vietnamese immigrant father, planning to marry a Mexican immigrant girlfriend next year, will have little sense of the United Kingdom.

Already you can see the dominance of non-Hispanic white people, who today account for two-thirds of Americans, shaping up for dramatic collapse. Two-thirds today – but the census folks say they will be half the population in 2042 and 46 per cent by 2050. In the opposite trajectory, those who describe themselves as Hispanic, black, Asian and Native American will increase in proportion from about a third now to 54 per cent by 2050. Hispanics alone will make up 30 per cent of the nation. This is a new revolution – one of the most far-reaching changes in a country's racial and ethnic make-up in history, every bit as dramatic as the huge influx of Italian, Irish and Eastern European immigrants that transformed the US in the early twentieth century.

The shift in majority status from non-Hispanic whites, who have enjoyed the dominant position since the gang who sailed in the *Mayflower* arrived in New England and survived that first winter, is going to have profound implications. In the long term, it may well lead to a sea-change in the country's understanding of its politics and culture, but already, I would argue, it is leading to a new sense of its relationships with the outside world. For this reminted version of America is going to look with a much broader vision of its own heritage on the various outside powers competing for attention.

To put it bluntly: the Hugh Grant stuff cuts no ice with these brown folk. And this – fundamentally – is why the Foreign affairs Committee was right and the sentimentalists of the British press are wrong. Change has come. Though the extent of future change, the kind of change that sees Matt Frei as happy to be German as English in Boise, is an open question and an interesting one. It is here that the echoes of the special relationship may or may not count for something in the coming decades. For America has a choice to make. It is not a choice between being cosy with the English or not cosy with the English. It is a much more interesting and profound choice about the kind of nation that Americans themselves want to have, and the choice impacts directly on us.

America is mad as hell. The recession – which the *Sunday Times* economics editor Anatole Kaletsky eye-catchingly suggests could have a longer-term and deeper impact on America than 9/11 – has knocked for six some of the central pieces of American political furniture. I accept that; other books will focus on what happened and why. My interest is in one area: America's sense of itself and of what it means to be American. Shortly after he became President, a friend of mine asked Barack Obama whether he believed in American exceptionalism. "Hot Damn," he replied, "the USA rules and always will." No, of course he didn't say that. In fact, he didn't say anything much, expect that he was sure Greeks believed in Greek exceptionalism and he regarded America in the same way. This is a cop-out. The general view across the political divide in the US is that the nation, if not divinely invested with the purpose of improving humanity, is or should be mighty well qualified to do the job. The right stresses strength and the left stresses example but both sides in American politics are pretty sure that America is qualitatively different from the rest of the industrialised world. And at the heart of the enterprise is the American Creed. Now that creed – hard work, old-style religion etc – the pioneer creed upon which America is based, comes from the *Mayflower*.

There is a lively historical controversy about the motives of the original *Mayflower* passengers. Part of the reason they made the ghastly journey west was religious persecution, but partly as well it was an economic decision – they thought they could make a totally new life. But the central, most important point is that these people were not (as the failed Virginia settlers had been) aristocrats out to make a buck. They were the dispossessed. That is America's seed-corn: to have nothing and gamble everything. The boat arrived in Plymouth, Massachusetts, and the character of America was forged in the horror of the early efforts to stay alive, the mistreatment by and mistreatment of the Native Americans, and the long tear-strewn and hope-strewn march west. If America is an idea as much as a place, then the idea was born in the *Mayflower* and honed by the future generations who would throw the British out and forge the strongest country on earth. There are around 600 American families who trace their ancestry to the *Mayflower*. They are the slim but sinewy trunk of the multi-branched tree.

Or are they? This is what America has to decide. The exceptionalist places the creed and the attachment to a set of values, a narrative, at the heart of the nation. The waves of immigrants who arrived in New York harbour in the nineteenth and twentieth centuries were almost all of them arriving blind, in the sense that they could have no conception of what the future held for them. They were, generally, banned from having any kind of employment already arranged. They were to be social virgins. It was not quite *Mayflower* conditions but their lives were, in many cases, pretty awful. For modern-day immigrants, from Benin or South Korea or Mexico, life is much easier. A pre-arranged job is often required rather than banned. But the idea is still that when you arrive in America you sign up for something, and something more than just the basic citizenship ceremony. You sign up for the *Mayflower*. For individualism tempered by community support, for Puritanism tempered by a belief in happiness. You leave your baggage at home or, if you bring it, you leave it largely unpacked. This, of course, is the opposite of multiculturalism. It does not celebrate the traditions and the whacky beliefs of your forefathers. It does not even begin to toy with the idea that you should live in your own community and speak your mother tongue and never mix with the rest of the nation. That would be un-American.

But here is the issue. If America becomes steadily more heterogeneous – and that is a given – does it also lose sight of the history of how it came to be great? In particular, does it lose sight of the links with Europe and that creed that has been handed down from generation to generation. To put it crudely: when white America dies, will the *Mayflower* go down with it? And white America will die, in the sense of being the dominant force in the nation, and it will do so quite soon; of that there seems to be no real doubt. Change, you could argue, has actually not yet come – but it is around the corner. It is an interesting fact that the demographic revolution I have referred to in this chapter is also going to have a generational impact. White folks will be old. Already, nearly half of all American children under five come from minority communities. By the middle of the century, more than 60 per cent of American children will not be white. This matters in all kinds of ways, and, being Americans, most will see it as an opportunity to be seized. Nonetheless, this seizing of the future might involve a break with the past – and the ghosts of the past – that the nation has never before contemplated. America is already a tad hazy about its former greatest ally. A survey a few years ago found that many Americans thought the United Kingdom was somewhere off the Persian Gulf. But the real change comes when the nation has made a complete ethnic break with its past. That is when the old Protestant work ethic, the old sense of individualism, the old attachment to inequality and harshness that went alongside that individualism, might all begin to fall away. Where does it leave the special or essential relationship? Where does it leave Winston Churchill? Winston who?

On the other hand, perhaps a little distance might be beneficial. Shorn of the constant disappointment of the relationship, finally freed from the expectation that the President is going to call and ask our permission to sneeze or invade somewhere, perhaps this is the moment that we can relax and begin to get on better. Perhaps, too, we can escape from the self-disgust, the self-loathing even, that is brought on by the strain of trying to maintain to ourselves that our relationship is equal when we know in our hearts that it is not. And that escape could be consequential, allowing an insouciance to develop about some American traits and habits, particularly domestic oddities like execution or religiosity, that at the moment get us so steamed up because we are not influencing these matters in the way that the Yanks seem so effortlessly to invade and influence our own popular culture, even our language.

The former controller of Radio Four, Mark Damazer, sent me a note years ago complaining about my use on air of the phrase "going forward", a phrase you hear regularly now, especially among business people. My colleague John Humphrys carries on the battle – if he asks you how you are, do not, on pain of death, reply "good" – and the battle might or might not be one worth having (I will address it in detail in Chapter Ten); my point is that we would be more relaxed about our relationship with America, more cheerfully unruffled, if we did not have in the back of our minds the vague, unformed but powerful notion that we have to protect ourselves against a partner bent on abusing partnership and getting the better of us at every turn.

Chapter Three

The reason our interests have so often coincided is not merely expediency but because we stand upon the same hallowed moral ground: an enduring belief in the sanctity of the individual, a commitment to representative government, common religious traditions, and an unfaltering dedication to the rule of law.
Margaret Thatcher, the James Bryce Lecture,
London, 1996

BARACK OBAMA'S SPEECH to the 2008 Democratic Convention was widely regarded as a triumph, one of the crucial stepping stones to the presidency. The event was on a scale no one had attempted before; and it could have been an expensive and embarrassing flop. First, the Democrats abandoned the conference centre and its cavernous interior for a proper piece of space, the 76,000-seater Denver Broncos football stadium. Next, they constructed a backdrop in the centre of the field that brought ancient Greece and the Greek word *hubris* to the state of Colorado. Raised on a giant stage there was a wide corridor of Doric columns leading back to a faux building that looked suspiciously like the White House. All of it was laminated plywood. Pretentious? Just a little, giggled the right, and waited for the edifice to come tumbling down. But when Obama strode out on the stage and walked his comfortable walk to the microphone, he managed to turn in one of the best performances of his campaign; he dwarfed the columns, metaphorically at least, and did much to unite the fractured party behind his just-won candidacy.

All of this I remembered as I caught the train from Euston to Liverpool two years later. A year was up since my return to Britain and it was party time. From around the nation, the faithful, the not-so-faithful and the downright rebellious were gathering for the first modern coalition conference season – all of them hoping to second a composite motion on live TV, or at least get invited to the Mumsnet lunch with the free booze. Some of them, perhaps dimly remembering Obama's triumph in the Denver Broncos football stadium, were imagining Doric columns of their own. I went to the first of the gatherings, the Liberal Democrats'. It was the first major political meeting I had attended since Denver in 2008: where, in addition to Obama's triumph on the final night, we had coped with the momentous fallout from his efforts to win, culminating in the floor-vote in which Hillary Clinton had been forced, finally and symbolically, to admit defeat and endorse the presidential bid of Barack Obama.

From Denver to Liverpool: progress or what? Well, the comparison is not wholly ridiculous. What do the meetings of the party faithful in two broadly similar political parties, in two major cities not normally on the beaten track for most of the nation, tell us about the way Brits and Americans see themselves politically? More importantly, what do they tell us about the way we see ourselves (and each other) socially and politically?

Conferences and conventions have both changed over the years from being smoke-filled affairs of great immediate consequence to having a much broader-brush influence. For the Democrats, there is still the folk memory of the calamity of Chicago in 1968; rioters on the streets and utter confusion in the hall, as the various factions battled for control of the party on the issue of Vietnam. The whole thing was a debacle – a television strike meant that people in the hall had little idea of the violence going on outside. When taped pictures started to be played it was too late for the leaders to intervene. Pandemonium ensued. One senator screamed that Gestapo tactics were being used on the streets of Chicago and the city's Mayor, Richard Daley (also a Democrat), responded by leaping to his feet, shaking his fists and hurling abuse – including what commentators referred to as a "crude sexual accusation" – at the elderly senator. The Democratic Party had managed to tear itself apart only weeks before the election, with the result that Richard Nixon strolled home, and the rest – as they say – is history.

In the UK, we don't have a Chicago equivalent but we have had some pretty wicked battles at our party conferences – and that used to be the whole point, at least on the left; these were the crucibles where policy emerged. Even the Conservatives have had their semi-Chicago moments: Iain Duncan Smith's last conference in charge ("the quiet man... is turning up the volume") was said by many who attended to have been poisonous from beginning to end and in many respects sealed the fate of the leader. Conferences used to be powerful tools. Some parties gave them more policy zip than others but the need to impress the conference, to tickle the tummies of the party faithful (metaphorically or otherwise) drove generations of politicians to the windswept British seaside. If you wanted to get immersed in your chosen party you had to go. And you still do. On both sides of the Atlantic, even in the age of Facebook and Twitter, there is a desire to commune and a function in meeting. And an odd similarity – even a sameness – in the people doing the meeting and the way they approach their tasks.

First the Democrats of 2008. Boy, did they care about what was going to happen. Remember Hillary Clinton and Barack Obama had been fighting tooth and nail for months to win their party's backing as the candidate. Obama delivered the early blow at Iowa, but Clinton had fought back and in the summer had really achieved something of a moral draw, though perhaps ultimately lacking the strength to beat him. It looked as if she would have no option but to accept defeat – the nomination was his and would come at the convention. Standing outside the conference centre on the first day, I gathered together a few Clinton supporters (she had not yet formally conceded) for what I thought might be a gentle reflection on what might have been. What emerged was a picture of bubbling resentment and a desire to head off the inevitable Obama victory, at all costs. Our interview was so bizarre that it was largely unusable. One woman told me that she had once been raped, "but I will feel more violated today, if Hillary Clinton is not nominated as our candidate!"

So park the idea that modern American conventions are balloon-filled confections with no passion and no meaning. There was plenty of passion in Denver.

And when the decision came – the moment for Obama to take the crown – the Clinton people forced a count from the floor of the various states and the way they had voted. Eventually, when it got to New York (Clinton's state), she announced that she wanted to end the process and endorse Obama. Cue balloons and tears and screaming and hugging. I remember more than anything the physicality of that moment: the place stank of sweat and stale food; we were packed in like old-style football supporters on the stands; Hillary Clinton had to be virtually carried to the centre of the hall – they could not get her close to the podium so they brought a microphone to her. You could see – actually see – power draining from the Clinton family and into the usurper. People fainted.

And the convention had done its job.

Conventions are political tornadoes; they suck in the politics of the last four years, mash them to bits, then chuck the fragments into the distant recesses of the nation just in time for the election of the new president. They are staggering in their intensity. And even if the speeches from the floor can seem a tad formulaic there is plenty happening away from the spotlight, plenty to experience that tells you what's going on, if you only have the eyes to see and the ears to hear. An example: rushing out to find the BBC mobile cabin as one session was drawing to a close (it must have been mid-evening on that warm, late, summer night), I got lost and stumbled into an unfamiliar car park. Secret Service men barred my way, and from a side road that passed into the conference centre, a mass of outriders and four-wheel-drive wagons emerged with very large chaps holding very serious guns sitting in the open side doors, alert and agile, like helicopter winch-men. Behind them came a limousine, and through the open window, as it passed me, I looked in and met the gaze of three faces: Mrs Obama and her daughters, Sasha and Malia. African-American children had been at the very bottom of the pile in American society until only decades ago. They had been treated with contempt particularly in the South. And now here they were, bemused and surely wondering at this weird turn their lives were taking, but nonetheless aware suddenly that the state had taken them to its bosom. Every sinew of America's mighty security machine would now be used to protect these black children. I found it oddly moving, in fact, rather more moving than seeing

Obama himself receive the nomination. After all, there had been prominent black politicians before. But never had there been a black family so centrally placed in the structure of America, so intimately held in the palm of America's hand. They were gone in a flash but that very brief encounter left a lasting impression.

And so to Liverpool. And in the getting there, an Englishness that seems in one sense almost too obvious to mention but that goes to the heart of us and them. We travelled there by train, of course. And in doing so, we moved reasonably effortlessly from the very centre of one city (Euston Station in London) to the very centre of another (Liverpool Lime Street). These geographical facts – the locations of these two stations – have political and social consequences. Americans, when they gave up the railways as a means of travel towards the end of the last century, also gave up on stations and, to an extent, on inner cities. Nobody arrived in Denver by train for the Democrats in 2008; all either drove or flew.

And in flying they assisted the economy of the out-of-town airport, which glitters in isolation at the end of a long road and from which you cannot even see the city. Liverpool Lime Street, with its central location, bustling with short-distance commuters, grannies en route to families in Penzance and Liberal Democrats arriving from Southampton, is not really an equivalent to this. To be sure, both are places where thousands of people congregate and many have travelled long distances to get there, but the overall impression at Denver Airport, unlike at Liverpool Lime Street, is of homogeneity. Gift shops dispense Colorado tat to tourists and business travellers alike. And if you don't want it and fancy visiting a shop that is not in the airport, you would have to drive for half an hour to get into town.

The late Tony Judt, who was London-born but taught at New York University, used to say that trains (and particularly stations) had a social importance that was not properly understood. In *Ill Fares the Land*, his attack on the modern Western world's obsession with the individual, Judt wrote: "Airports typically (and irritatingly) linger well past the onset of aesthetic or functional obsolescence... but railway stations built a century or even a century and a half ago... not only inspire affection: they are aesthetically appealing and they work."

It led Judt to a conclusion of great relevance when studying us and them: "any country without an efficient rail network is in crucial respects 'backwards'."

Judt's point with regard to my journey from London to Liverpool is that the journey saw us mix with local people in both places, in buildings that were genuinely community spaces with strong local heritages. Our journey was made on a mode of transport that is – even on privatised Virgin Trains – essentially a social service. The line from London to Liverpool will never close. The air route from Washington to Denver is only as strong as the commercial case for keeping it open.

Judt may be right or wrong, but the case he makes for America's transport choices having had implications for society is irrefutable. If the old gateway to the West, and self-proclaimed largest and busiest terminal in the world, St Louis Union Station, was still a station rather than a tourist shopping mall, the centre of the city would still be thriving rather than hollowed out and dead as it largely is. And folks could say "Meet me under the clock at Union Station", rather than "Pick me up in the car at the Gateway Multimodal Transportation Center", which, in all seriousness, is what the modern station is called. To which the lazy response is: "Have you not looked at an atlas and noticed that America is, like, *big*?" Well, it is, and some routes are plainly unfeasible by even the fastest trains. But Americans have given up trying: St Louis is only 300 miles from one of America's most important economic and political hubs, Chicago. But the train (one a day) takes more than five and a half hours to get there. It is of use only to tourists and people who have taken too many drugs to be able to find their cars. London is about 180 miles from Liverpool and you can do it in two and a half hours, with a train every hour for most of the day.

Barack Obama noticed this and drew it to the nation's attention when he became President. We should build high-speed lines, he told Americans, and while he didn't quite go the whole Judt distance, he seemed to be suggesting that European-style rail travel might be a generally civilising force. The reaction was interestingly hostile. Mr Obama's train idea was one of the early signs, to many Americans, that he did not entirely *get* the nation he had been elected to run. I remember years ago reading about a plan to build a railway line to a popular East Coast holiday destination. It was scuppered by the locals who complained that trains would bring the kind of people who went on public transport, and those people were always bad news. Americans have come to associate public transport with desperation – economic, social, often personal. The idea of Liverpool Lime Street does not fill them with joy. And this goes deeper than simply convenience; the idea that freedom is buttressed by cars and planes as well as guns and constitutions has become an American myth. Nobody arriving with me in Liverpool would have thought that. We are herded around our small island cheek by jowl with folks to whom we have not been introduced, and we may occasionally feel annoyed or uncomfortable or close to screaming "Get off my foot" but we do not really feel unfree. Americans, out of their cars and airports, do.

And once we get to Liverpool we are allowed to be eccentric – free – in ways Americans cannot quite manage. When I arrived at my Liverpool hotel there was a man in reception asking for a blanket. "Are you cold?" the staff asked. "No, it's for my dog!"

That exchange would never have happened in Denver.

In many ways going to Liverpool allowed me to re-establish a link with an England that was reassuringly familiar. All that early talk of discombobulating extra security at the Liberal Democrats' conference was rubbish. True, the party had achieved some measure of power for the first time in 65 years and we live in an age of terrorist threats, but the security seemed to me to be no more intense than I remembered it from years before. The passes might have been a little more professional – and they were checked twice on the way in – but Fort Knox it was not. What had changed, and this is surely a reflection of a change in society rather than anything to do with the Lib Dems, was the attitude towards health and safety, or Health and Safety, I should say. My attempt to take a cup of coffee down the escalator in the centre of the conference centre was greeted with horror: You must have a lid, the security man said, or I cannot let you pass. It was the same in the main hall. A pause to greet a friend on a stairway up to the top seats would be pounced on by anxious men with wiggly wires in their ears: *no blocking of the escape routes,* they would hiss insistently as the speaker droned on. But there are only fifteen people in the hall! No matter, rules is rules.

In America, it is not like that at the party conventions. The security is tighter and the queues to get in longer but, once in, you can roam pretty well unmolested. The escalators are packed with portly conservative radio talk show hosts bringing snacks of reheated meat and grease down to their lairs in the basement. Everyone eats and drinks all the time at these events. And it's not a pretty sight. I met a vegetarian woman at the Democrats' in Denver literally in tears as she searched for something she could consume; we were on the concessions floor of the Denver Broncos football stadium and she had been walking in a straight line looking for tofu. What she had not clocked was that the stadium was so massive, and the curve of its walkways so slight, that you got little sense that you were walking in a circle, and so she had in fact gone round and round in circles, and past the same hotdog stand several times without realising it. She had thought she was in purgatory with a literally never-ending vista of the same ghastly food outlets.

Ah, a football stadium. Now this is another difference. American conventions are held only every four years and they are very big events indeed. There is no pretence that the speeches are aimed at the folks in the hall. Our conferences are still intimate enough for effective and clever speeches to garner real appreciation and real impact as the audience sit a few feet in front of the speaker. In American conventions, the distance between the podium and the audience is so huge that no such relationship is possible. The audience's enthusiasm is taken for granted. These people are a prop, not a sounding board. A congressional candidate I knew addressed the Democrats in Boston in 2004. His local Virginia party delegates turned up with posters and screamed whenever he made a point during his ten-minute speech; everyone in the rest of the hall chatted among themselves or tucked into their food. The Virginia TV clip would show him and the "enthusiasm" of his people. It was entirely fake, like a councillor from Budleigh Salterton bussing 500 locals to a British party conference and having them stand on their seats when he spoke.

In contrast, the informality of the British system allows for speeches that matter, for audience reactions that count.

American political dialogue at party conventions takes place in the margins, and somewhat marginal figures take part. In Denver in 2008, no one was able to say, "I am joined now by Barack Obama and let me begin by asking you about the fake marble columns…" It was inconceivable that the real players should take part in any debate that was not pre-rehearsed. One of the disasters of modern American media life has been the almost blanket ability of the political class to avoid serious forensic cross-questioning. The only person who manages it is the comedian Jon Stewart, on whose show politicians go in order to appear cool or sell books. Nowhere in Denver was anyone seriously tested. If it had been Britain, both Hillary Clinton and Barack Obama would have been on the *Today* programme; to turn it down would have been seen as an abdication of responsibility. In Liverpool, all the main speakers performed on the stage and then expected to have their speeches subjected to what we call *stress tests* in the real world. Danny Alexander, the Liberal Democrat Chief Secretary to the Treasury, had (in his speech) called tax avoidance immoral, and was duly attacked in the studios afterwards for avoiding it himself on a housing transaction (a charge he denies). When I talked to the leader Nick Clegg on *Today*, we made space not just for one question about what seemed to be the rather dodgy ground of the morality of tax avoidance, but for several, in an exchange that went on for minutes and resulted in newspaper head-lines the following day. This is the British way. We are, in this respect, more serious than Americans, but also psychologically more able to cope with the idea that political leaders are, at best, groping after answers that they themselves half understand and half shrink from. In Liverpool, no one pretended that all was well, either with the Liberal Democrats or with the nation. In Denver, the Democrats had to be portrayed as stupendously ready for power, and the nation as quite obviously ripe for improvement at the drop of the Democrats' hat. There is a lack of subtlety in American political discourse that drives the peculiar fact that, in a nation hugely united and hugely successful in so many areas, the recent history of its politics has been ghastly, even frightening, for many Americans who cannot understand why so many people in the country – flyers of the same flag and singers of the same anthem – hate each other so much.

Well, it's the interviews, stupid. Or the lack of them. American politics is, in many ways, strangely polite. Elderly senators respect each other across party lines with embarrassing displays of octogenarian affection. Nobody gets interviewed by John Humphrys. Nobody is subjected to Prime Minister's Questions. So when the going gets tough and there are real issues to thrash out, the politicians have tended to play nice and leave it to the folks at home to play nasty. It is the opposite of the British system, where decent polite people tell the politicians to be less confrontational. Perhaps the rough-house stuff around the fringes of Liverpool creates the space for ordinary Britons to feel that there is no need to question their neighbours' patriotism or parentage in the manner of the ugly rows that have convulsed American politics in recent years. In Denver, everyone was united and flag-waving but something was missing: the Clinton supporter who had been raped could not make her points on the convention floor. The candidates themselves would not have it out with their opponents in the Republican party on morning radio. In a later chapter, I suggest that part of the reason for this is the concern Americans have for freedom of speech, even if this freedom negates democracy. They have fostered a climate in broadcasting where anything goes, and this has affected not just the volume of insults

and shouting underneath the smooth top tier of politicians (who avoid any but friendly broadcasters), but
also the psychology of media consumption – either you
subscribe to the partial view of the world put forward
by these news channels or else you regard them all as
inherently biased, and thus suspect. It is ugly and sad
and it results in our politics being superior to theirs in
this respect.

They have also come horribly unstuck over money
in politics. I have never subscribed to the lazy view
that American political debate is all about balloons and
froth and is controlled by men with dollars in their eyes
and identical sets of basic interests, whether they call
themselves Democrats or Republicans. American politics is a seething cauldron of ideas and genuine clashes
between real alternatives. But: there is a legitimate and
reasonable view that the need to raise money to fight
campaigns – zillions of dollars even for a two-bit Senate
campaign – tends to lend politicians, or sell them, to
those who can pay these sums. Thus American politics
looks like something of a glorious dust-up, but might
be, on closer examination, rather less than that. The
election of 2012 will see a billion dollars spent by each
of the two presidential candidates. That money has to
come from somewhere. And somewhere will want a
return. Part of the reason why the US national debt is

so mountainous is that America simply does not like paying tax and American politicians do not like asking for it, even from the very rich. The reason is more than natural reticence: every two years in congressional elections, the politicians need to come cap in hand to the wealthiest individuals and corporations and try to get their campaigns funded. They have to keep these people sweet, even when they know it makes no long-term economic sense.

Political meetings are about more than policies, ideas, debate. They have a physical side to them; they are about power and power relationships, and in themselves they illustrate some of those relationships. Coming by train matters. The distance from the stage to the audience matters. The sights outside the conference centre matter. And the strength of the stress tests on ideas and people also matter. Becoming president involves massive organisational ability, stellar chutzpah, a killer instinct, but not, it seemed in Denver, any real ability to have thought through what you want to do and defend it in public against persistent hostile questioning. And money matters too. America is not run, as conspiracy theorists suppose, by shadowy powerful forces who control the will of the masses. But there is a disconnect between the top and the bottom: the Tea Party movement has illustrated, dramatised, that gap. The Supreme Court ruling that corporate money can now be used to fund campaigns directly (funnelled through organisations so that you will not be able to see which organisation is funding which cause) is a potential body-blow to democracy and frankly I cannot see it standing. But fundamentally, as both the Obama campaign and the Tea Party showed, America can still be energised from the bottom up.

But they have to work on it and they could learn from the way British politics is carried out in the 21st century. In Liverpool, it was open season on the Liberal Democrats and they, and we, were the better for it. I am a fan of American politics and I certainly don't subscribe to the lazy view that there are no real choices on offer there; but the journey to Liverpool is a reminder that Britain is a grittier place at the top – we have our political debates inducted with full vigour and involving the most senior politicians. We do not always admire them but we do use them to give us the space to get on with other things. In America the sanitisation of top politics has left an ugly space under the rock where nasty creepy crawlies can fester and plot.

I have to admit that one of my efforts in Denver to speak to ordinary people – to hear from the grass-roots – was a notable disaster. During the Hillary Clinton acceptance speech, I had been squeezed right into the centre of the hall, next to a distinguished-looking black man. I could not see his face as the momentous announcement was made that Barack Obama was to be the party's choice of presidential candidate. My head was pressed into this man's back as we moved – like people in those old-fashioned football stands – gradually towards the exit, and I decided that when we got to the doors I would ask this fellow what went through his mind as the announcements were made. He looked old enough to have known real oppression at the hands of white Americans, and his parents certainly would have lived lives curtailed and poisoned by racism. So we got to the door and I tapped him on the shoulder and he turned...

It was Sir Trevor McDonald.

Denver was like that. Glamorous, but not quite getting to the heart of the matter. Liverpool was far less glamorous, and the heart of the matter far easier to reach. This is Englishness – Britishness perhaps – at its best and Americanness at its worst.

Chapter Four

Americans are optimistic, friendly, inquisitive, practical-minded. They find it difficult to believe that progress is not inevitable. They do not easily accept the right to reserve and privacy; they assume that if two men meet the natural thing is for them to exchange experiences. They have a distrust of theory. What interests them is the ability to apply an idea to the solution of a problem; and they reserve their supreme respect for men of the type of Ford rather than men of the type of Theodore Richards.

Harold Laski, *The American Democracy*, 1949

THEODORE WHO? HE appears – googled – to be the first American to win the Nobel Prize for Chemistry. He suffered from depression and had two sons, both of whom killed themselves. So Harold Laski has a point here. Most Americans would indeed, socially and psychologically, tend to sympathise more with Ford. This wonderfully fusty piece of prose, penned

by the doyen of English left-wing academics just after
the war, brings home the full extent of the cultural
separateness of Johnnie American (he is described
here as you might describe a spaniel), but also the
constancy of our view of him and its essential truth.
Laski's description, up to and including Ford and
poor old Theodore Wotsit, is as valid today as it was
then. Laski is best known in Britain as a commentator on and critic of the great Labour government
of 1945 – he was himself a chairman of the Labour
Party and a dominant voice of the left, cited as a big
influence by, among others, Ralph Miliband, David
and Ed's communist dad. But this view of America
and Americans came before the left turned against
America. Much of what they admired – modernity
and efficiency and the ability of every man to achieve
his potential – was there to be seen in America and
should still be there today if only Americans let it
happen. Americans, said Laski, did not suffer from
the human contradiction "of being either a nobleman
without the means to live the noble life, or being a
merchant or a peasant, and finding, even if he was
successful, that these circles of social life to which he
might aspire were beyond his hope of entry". They
are, in other words, free of class. That characterisa-
tion, with a little tinkering, still holds true.

But Laski's American is also (and I wonder whether he noticed this when he came back from Yale to teach at the LSE in the 1920s) rather free of, well, fun. There has been a suspicion of the unconventional in American life since the founding of the republic and this suspicion, it seems to me, is what lies at the heart of their problem with humour. Laski suggests – rightly maybe – that the stress on teamwork in order for the various goals of American life to be met when the nation was being set up is the heart of the problem. You can be a rugged individualist in certain areas but when it comes to cultural togetherness you have to toe the line. This is not a problem we Brits have.

So although Americans can be funny, although they can be quick-witted and sympathetic and worldly and wise, they cannot, in the field of humour, be British. I spoke at a small lunch shortly after coming back to London and, as I was leaving, a friend of mine who'd come along caught up with me and said: "You were rubbish. Truly awful. You've obviously never done it before. You need to practise." It was a sweet thing to say. As all of you who are British will immediately recognise, he was being highly complimentary in that good old British manner. (At least that's what I understood – Oh God, was I wrong? Please call me, friend, and confirm.)

I liked what he said, anyway. And it reminded me that the earnestness of American life was something I could never really celebrate. Americans who think you have done well will say: "You did great!" They will smile too, in case the message is unclear. There will be no deadpan and no room for misunderstanding. If you do badly they will walk away, embarrassed. In Britain, it's as if we are all sharing a long and not always particularly funny joke – a shaggy dog story whose end is not yet in sight but whose perambulations make us titter and feel that we know each other, and we like it that way. In our interactions in the drizzle – mordantly humorous, bleakly ironic – we celebrate life in our own twisted way.

Sometimes too twisted.

Crossing the road in south London shortly after arriving back, dazed from an early start at my new place of work, I slightly misjudged the distance between me and an oncoming car. This mistake could have inconvenienced the driver but only marginally. He might have had to take his foot off the accelerator but would have missed me easily if he had continued at his previous speed.

But he didn't. He speeded up! He still missed, I am delighted to say, because even at my advanced age I can still sidestep when necessary, but his intention was clear. He wanted to kill or maim the person crossing the road in front of him – or at least terrify the living daylights out of him.

This is not an isolated incident. You can see it on any street in any town in Britain. Drivers (and cyclists) speed up to make a point.

In America they do not do this. Barring Las Vegas – where a large proportion of drivers are desperate folks on their way home to explain to their wives that the last dollar has gone and they can't afford toilet paper any more – there is nowhere in the US where you would expect this to happen. American drivers slow down for pedestrians. They drive gently, respectfully. They do not employ irony behind the wheel.

At the end of the street where we lived in Washington, there was a four-way stop, a common road intersection in America. The first person to arrive at the crossroads has priority – everyone must stop but can continue their journey in the order in which they arrived at the junction. It works. In fact, the only slight nuisance at these halts is the extreme politeness – *no, no, after you* – that can cause four cars simply to stop and wait for each other. No matter. I have come to miss the gentility of the four- way stop. It would not work in Camberwell. Nor in Brussels, where I lived years ago and where the rules of the road are designed to make life as difficult and dangerous as possible for passengers and the less-aggressive drivers. In Brussels they have a thing called *priorité à droite*. Folks arriving in a lane of traffic from the left have the right of way. They emerge without warning into the path of oncoming traffic. It makes for accidents and jerky, nervy driving. It is one of the reasons why Belgians hate each other with such unalloyed passion. The civilised Europeans, masters of the post-modern ironic universe, keepers of the flame of ancient learning, bash headlong into each other's cars with murderous rancour at any opportunity. The Americans hold back.

American gentility is a paradox, to put it mildly. There are aspects of American life that are bracing to the point of brutality: their health system, even post-Obama; their income disparities; their adherence (at least in the South) to a Christian faith that owes as much to the Old Testament as to the New; the mad, gaudy shoutiness of their politics in the modern age. But along with the harshness at the level of public life, there is a civility in normal suburban relations that Britain simply cannot match. Pervading every American equivalent of a British market town there is a calm and a harmony that puts one in mind of, well, Britain in the 1950s.

How do they do it? Guns and religion play a part. There is a yearning in the American psyche for well-disciplined order. Having no sense of irony leaves room for an overdeveloped sense of right and wrong. Relativism in the US is a love of relatives. But the greatest cause of America's calm is its patriotism. And not the type we normally notice. The American patriotism we all know too well – the flag and the flummery surrounding it – is only the tip of the nation-loving iceberg. The lower levels – the really solid levels on which the whole is built – are in communities in which they really do believe that "we are all in this together".

Truly believing that phrase makes a real difference. It causes people not just to pick up litter but not to drop it in the first place. It enables neighbourhoods to watch out for crime without any formal watch system being in place. It encourages volunteer fire services (our local service in Washington was wholly staffed by volunteers), and above all it prevents drivers from speeding up to hit pedestrians because... Well, why would you?

I freely admit that when we first came back to London, we wondered how people survived the city. The question never arose when I lived here as a student in the 1980s and as a youngish adult at various times since then. But after a decade away, and a return with young children and a more, shall we say, mature outlook on life, the capital city of my homeland seemed oddly frightening. I felt like a Kansas rube arriving in Manhattan in the 1970s. Your first thought is: *Vibrant!;* your second: *Help!*

Of course, modern Manhattan is now as peaceful as Nether Wallop. With New York taking its place among the world's more tranquil large cities – no murders at all in some weeks – much of the madness seems to have crossed the Atlantic. Almost everywhere you go in London, you are surrounded by deranged, dangerous people. After finishing my *Today* programme shift, I normally go home on the bus. The 148 is probably more frequent and certainly more comfortable than it would have been ten years ago but the people on the bus seem no happier. And when you step off it, you are in a land of almost comedic troubles. Walking home from the bus stop one morning, I paused to get money out of a cashpoint and found myself suddenly surrounded by sweaty, panting policemen. They were chasing someone, and they all piled into a café where the man might have been. A crowd gathered to watch the sport, several yelling encouragement, it wasn't clear to whom: the police or the man they were chasing. I pocketed my money and dashed. This scene would be unimaginable in the centres of most American cities. Outside the ghettos of the big cities, you will never, in America, see such street action.

And if you did, there would be a fuss. What strikes me on returning to Britain is how jaded we all are at the casual, low-level semi-violence that surrounds us. Interestingly, this is not new. The former Commissioner of the Metropolitan Police, Lord Blair, has written about the levels of violence that police officers come across in modern Britain. You would expect him to report that they are increasing. In fact, he says they are on the decrease. I find this perplexing because he should know. As should Sir Hugh Orde of the Association of Chief Police Officers, who privately took me to task once for suggesting that America seemed more peaceful that Britain. Perhaps the answer is that the kind of behaviour I find unsettling on returning to London is not really seen by today's police as violent. It is not even antisocial in any meaningful sense. But to me this behaviour is still odd and dysfunctional in a society where people ought really to be rubbing along.

An example: at Victoria Station in London the other day, a man – unremarkably dressed in jeans and sweat-shirt, in his thirties – was trying to stop one of those vehicles that pull trolleys back to their home when they've been left on the platform. He was hanging onto the last trolley – pulling it back and pushing it from side to side. The driver, feeling something wasn't right, thought he'd hit someone and stopped. When he realised this was not the case, he drove on, with the young man glaring at him. The man then made a final run at the the snaking line of trolleys and fell off the last one, turned abruptly and walked off into dusk. It was five o'clock in the evening. Was he drunk? Was he trying to say something? Was it a cry for help? Is this English humour?

Pondering these questions, I sat on a bench in Victoria Street outside the station. I had an appointment with a cabinet minister in the nearby Department for Work and Pensions. I was early so I sat and waited. Big mistake. A man demanded money. Really demanded it: with malice. In Washington, there are beggars in the streets but most of them are polite. The panhandler outside the BBC office on M Street was rather pally – I used to bump fists with him every day. If he threatened me, or anyone, he'd be carted off.

But here in Hogarth's London, I am the one who must run. It strikes me as ironic – as I enter the relative safety of the Department for Work and Pensions – that no one in this building is armed. In a city way more dangerous than Washington – a city stuffed full of desperate characters – the guard at the door has nothing more than a pencil with which to defend himself. As they say in America: good luck with that.

As I mentioned at the beginning of the book, when I came home from America I wasn't expecting Britain to be easy. I knew that valet parking – handing your keys to a man outside a restaurant and getting the car returned to you when you leave for the equivalent of a fiver – would soon be a distant memory. I knew that wide open spaces, proper vistas without houses or silly Stone Age-style drawings of men with improbably large appendages, do not exist in the English countryside. I knew that Downing Street was as shabby as the White House is chic.

But nothing prepared me for the booze. Sometimes it seems as if everyone here is drunk. Now, here I should add an important proviso: perhaps it's me that's changed, not my country; when I lived here before leaving for the US, it is possible, I suppose, that everyone was drunk *but I didn't notice*. Perhaps I was too drunk myself. But live in Washington DC for the best part of ten years, and it becomes the most striking feature of the return to to this side of the pond: America is sober, Britain is legless.

On a train, a group of people sat behind me and (I do not exaggerate) discussed for a full hour, London to Oxford, the various ways in which they had been sick.

They were like Eskimos with snow: familiarity had bred a rich language to describe the subject. Subtle changes of colour, lumps, vomit venues: nothing was off-limits. Why should it be? This was a big part of their lives.

In America this conversation, among twenty-somethings on their way home from work, would be inconceivable. American college students drink. American drunks drink. But regular folk leading regular lives do not drink to excess. Biologists tell us that one of the attributes that separate humans from the rest of the animal kingdom is a sense of disgust. Animals lick their own sick. Humans recoil from it. Except in England on the train home.

One of the effects of this sobriety is to make the American equivalent of an English market town oddly peaceful in comparison. I am not claiming that America has no problems with booze among the young or among the general population at home behind the white picket fences, but when it comes to public drunkenness and the crime associated with it, mainstream middle-class America escapes the kind of scenes of puke-smelling, fist-filled mayhem that John Humphrys described for the *Today* programme recently after a night out in his home town of Cardiff.

When I lived in America and met Brits over on holiday, their comments were a constant refrain: "Wow, it seems so much gentler than we thought." Well, that's because it's sober. And let's face it, there are plenty of aspects of American life that are far more violent than ours, from capital punishment to relaxed gun owner-ship, to a deeply held belief (even after the experiences of recent years) that war is a legitimate and useful tool of foreign policy. America was created in violence and, fuelled by old-time religion, still has an occasional hankering for a shoot-out. But with booze in check, ordinary people in ordinary places can go about their lives unmolested. It still annoys me that my mum, during the last few years of her life, could not walk the streets of the city of Bath at night. Bath, of all places! Hardly the roughest of English cities. And not peopled by murderers of old ladies either. But at night it was infested with enough drink-filled yobbishness to make it unsafe for frail folk to go home from the cinema.

And yet... Part of me, the English part perhaps, secretly rather enjoys boozed-up Britain. Talking to my wife the other day about why our first year back here had been 100 per cent more wonderful than we thought it would be, we both agreed that part of the problem with life in America was, well, *the sobriety!*

An example: quite early on in our Washington adventure, we were asked to a party by a very senior and well-known CNN correspondent. The beau -monde of the Washington broadcasting scene would be there. We turned up expecting sophistication. They were drinking punch. "Well, alright, just one glass," we said, fully intending to have ten. It looked a touch lethal – the colour of cherryade and served in large glasses. Lips touched liquid. It was all we could do not to spit it out. It *was* cherryade.

There was no booze. We were at a party with some of the most knowledgeable and well-connected and successful people in Washington and they were drinking cherryade. Somehow the whole event felt babyish. When a conjurer came in to entertain us (seriously!) and managed to take people's watches off without them realising, we were past caring. In Britain your kids would be beyond this stuff – and on the drink in some cases – in their teens, but in sober, temperance America it's what passes for a good time.

This memory led to a deeper and more worrying thought: did we really have anything at all in common with any of the people we had thought were our American friends? Had the whole thing been just a little too goody two-shoes? Had those great fun evenings with Hank and Jo-Anne (names changed to protect the very innocent) actually been, at the deeper level of the soul, unsatisfying and shallow and uptight in a manner that allowed for no real connection to take place? Getting tipsy with friends, one of the great British pastimes, is perhaps a more important part of a well-lived life than we had realised.

There is also in America a weird cultural history of actually fearing alcohol. The disastrous legacy of the failed effort to ban it completely is the peculiar relationship between modern Americans and booze. I remember Stanley McChrystal, the boss of NATO forces in Afghanistan till he was sacked for "dissing" Barack Obama, telling me that one of the first things he was going to do when he got to Kabul was ban drinking in the officers' mess. At the time of this revelation, we were both standing at a bar near the Pentagon with beers in our hands. The idea that such relaxation, without drunkenness, could be acceptable when work is at hand is very difficult for Americans to grasp. Stanley was having a drink because he was resting. When he went to work he was dry.

A friend who worked for Sky News in Washington confirmed this approach. To get to his bureau he had to walk through the Fox News office – and to be friendly on his first day he called out that anyone who fancied a drink should come with him. It was lunchtime. He might as well have told the Fox folk that he was a socialist transvestite. He was worried, he told me later, that they were going to call the cops.

The truth is that I am, as the Americans say, conflicted. I am revolted by the booziness of Britain but comforted as well. The other day, Gary Richardson came into the *Today* studio at 7.25 to do the sport carrying a glass of white wine. I didn't bat an eyelid. Actually, it turned out to be apple juice but what the heck: we are home! And feeling tipsy with delight…

And returning to Britain reminds me that the face America shows to the outside world, while sober in the extreme, is often oddly and unnecessarily hostile. Customs officials in the UK greet visitors face to face. I am sure there are some horrible ones among them but the general intention is to be civil. Even those passengers subjected to the greatest scrutiny are met initially by a person into whose eyes they can stare. Not so in America. The signs at Washington Dulles Airport speak of welcome, and the movie you watch while you wait in the hour-long queue to be seen speaks of homely America, but when you get to the front, the homeliness is replaced by something else: let's call it an abundance of caution. The immigration officials tend to be former military men – they are usually men – of a somewhat prickly disposition. They are armed; each one of them carries a pistol. Why? Any dangerous passengers would presumably have revealed themselves on the plane, not waited for the arrivals lounge.

Even the woman barking orders at the queue is armed. The truth, of course, is that they are not expecting to use the weapons – the queues are much safer than they would be at Victoria Station – but everyone with any kind of crowd-control authority in America tends to carry a gun. It is not really meant to be threatening, and not many Americans would give it a second thought, but the image is not friendly. Nor is the physical set-up for your passport check: the official is higher than you and surrounded by a steel framed cubicle. I have met some quite amiable ones in my time, though generally when the talk gets to politics, as it does when they ask what I do for a living, their views are more Kansas than San Francisco. They are primarily there to keep bad guys out rather than let good guys in.

In both Europe and America, let's face it, the threat of violence in the modern age is low. When Hogarth really was prowling the streets of London, or when the Wild West was being won, it was commonplace. Now it's not. But efforts to parry what violence there is, whether that violence is organised or the result of individual human malice, diverge with the Atlantic. In America the forces of authority are ready for a fight and in some respects I think that makes America a rather more peaceful place to live. And yet that very readiness for a fight is tiresome and reminds you constantly of danger, real or exaggerated, around every corner, in every airport. Perhaps the British way is best, where jovial policemen chase the hooligans, the crowd cheers enigmatically, and on Victoria Station, it's every man for himself.

Chapter Five

THERE IS A RECKLESS energy in American public life, an energy that speaks of daring and winning, an energy that leaves us in the shade. You saw it with Stanley McChrystal, the ill-fated head of the NATO mission in Afghanistan, who crashed and burned in 2010 after inviting a journalist from *Rolling Stone* on a drunken weekend jaunt to Paris. As I mentioned in the last chapter, Stanley was very sober on duty but on this occasion, it seemed, not so sober off duty. In Paris, he let his guard slip. It was a moment of madness but not out of character; it was in fact a moment of madness in a life full of such moments, an American life packed with bravado and not always quite as thought through as it might have been. Before he went to Afghanistan, appointed by the incoming President Obama to shake up the effort and define and execute victory, I visited the General in his Washington home.

In his sitting room there was a severed arm.

I noticed it immediately; I am, after all, a trained observer. And although I am also a pretty broad-minded fellow, in my limited experience of life, severed arms and sitting rooms do not necessarily go together. But nobody around me mentioned it. I was with his Pentagon minders waiting to interview the great man, and we made small talk about the Washington weather: already warming up, we agreed.

I cracked. "What's with the arm?"

I should explain that the severed arm was sticking out of the kind of ornate frame you might choose for a watercolour. The arm looked real – like a prosthetic limb. On closer inspection the oddity was compounded: in the hand there was a mobile phone.

The General entered, and explained: "The guys were fooling around. We went out to kill a sheik who had only one arm and we ended up getting the false arm but nothing else. That's not it," he adds, with a slight hint of wistfulness, "they just mocked that up for the joke. The phone was what gave his position away."

Stanley McChrystal was quite a character. In some respects he was out of central casting: big, with fierce eyes and weather-beaten skin. He looked every bit as fit as a Hollywood version of a special forces soldier. He ate one meal a day.

"That's not very good for you, is it?" I ventured.

"It's good for me."

When the General speaks, it's not a bark – this soldier has not seen a parade ground for many a long year – but a self-assured drawl. His voice is so quiet, in fact, that I have to strain to catch his words.

But it's worth the effort. America's military is often characterised as being more brawn than brain. In the past, some snooty Brits have suggested that Americans cannot really manage low-intensity wars because they're so wedded to their drones and nukes and kit. Literally, and metaphorically, they don't know when to take their helmets off, speak the local language, listen and learn.

Stanley McChrystal knew. The General was not an expert in counter-insurgency, nor did he claim to be. But he did know something about surgical strikes and the speedy use of human intelligence (and the signals sent out by mobile phones). He had a history of using massive force to great effect.

In Iraq (where the one-armed sheik got away), McCrystal is credited with killing dozens of key members of the insurgency. Until 2008 he led the Joint Special Operations Command, a shadowy group of soldiers and spies given the task of killing, capturing or otherwise neutralising senior members of Al Qaeda. Their biggest hit was Abu Musab al-Zarqawi, Al Qaeda's leader in Iraq. But he was far from the only target and far from the only scalp. There is a view that the success of the military surge in Iraq was due much more to the activities of General McChrystal's men than to the sheer number of boots on the ground.

And let us be plain: under his watch there were also allegations that those who were not killed were mistreated – tortured even – when brought back to base. He denies it but the allegation hangs around his neck.

He was certainly involved at every level in the operations he directed. At one of our meetings before he left for Afghanistan, I asked the General how close he had been to the nitty-gritty of soldiering in Iraq. His response spoke of his dedication to his art:

"I went out once a week with the guys. If they were going to pick someone off I liked to go along to keep in touch. They hated it, having me to look after!"

I doubted the last bit. They may have hated it, his men, but not because the General was a drag on their effort. Far from it: this man had standards and woe betide a junior officer who didn't match them.

When German NATO troops called in an air attack on stolen oil-filled tankers during his time in command, which killed a number of civilians in the process, McChrystal had trouble raising some of his

European colleagues on the phone. It turned out they were having a drink in the officers' mess. No longer: drinking in all NATO establishments in Afghanistan was quietly banned.

As I've said, it's not that the General is teetotal, but that he was in Afghanistan on business. Focus was his thing. This is the American way. There is something about the American character that rolls up its shirt-sleeves and ticks off tasks. It is not unthinking, this drive, but it does lead to an other-worldly relentless-ness. A British friend who went to Harvard remembers a trip he and his classmates took to China. While having a drink on the plane out, they decided that they would speak the Mandarin they were learning – and only Mandarin – once they woke to get off their night flight. My friend woke up a few hours later, having long forgotten this champagne-fuelled pact. His friends had forgotten nothing. Solemnly, they reached for their bags and assisted each other with the boarding cards, speaking only Mandarin. The British chap realised that when it came to seriousness of purpose, he would always be a loser at his chosen university.

But the flip side of this seriousness of purpose is an ability to go off the rails with quite spectacular, Roman-candle like luminosity. Poor Stanley McChrystal managed it with his *Rolling Stone* interview, which saw him summarily fired by the slow-to-anger Obama. F. Scott Fitzgerald's famous dictum that there are no second acts in American lives is most often quoted today as an example of grandiose falsehood. Of course there are second acts: America is full of reinvention, revivification, is it not? Well, it is, but those picking up the pieces after a disaster are often the later generations. People get busted in America. They fly so high and fall so far that the wreckage, to use the old plane crash cliché, is spread over a wide area. F. Scott Fitzgerald had a point.

In a sense Obama himself fits into this category. His campaign for office was the most spectacular success in recent American history. He overcame hurdles of race and politics and personality to seize the presidency. He raised staggering sums of money. The American system allows such triumphs. A friend of mine – a French commentator – is fond of telling his countrymen that there are two necessities if you are to stand for high office in France. First, you must be known. Secondly, you must stand. In Britain it is the same; because of the lack of primaries our politicians must be stewed in the juices of Westminster before finally becoming famous and truly powerful. In America the opposite is the case. First, you must stand. Secondly, you need to become known. This encourages – in all aspects of American life – an approach that suggests possibilities before it fears dangers. An approach that juts out the chin and puffs up the chest before searching for the umbrella and asking the insurer whether you are covered.

But the corollary of this boldness is the fact that Americans can fall on their faces and not really, truly, ever get up again. Take Obama. He is – in spite of being of mixed race – America's first black president and his presidency has been a disappointment to many of his most ardent supporters because he has failed to transform the nation as he had promised. That is the epitaph. Nothing he does or says will really outlive that simple fact (or semi-fact). Just as Reagan won the Cold War, or Bush senior messed up the economy, or Bush junior invaded Iraq, Obama will be left in the minds of future Americans as a piece of graffiti that contains the word black and the word disappointment. His second term could be a success. His health care reforms could eventually bed down in a way that produces grudging respect. But the early years will always mark him. In Britain we do not do this. Non-partisan Brits will look back on Lady Thatcher with a genuinely more nuanced view. The folk memory points out her failures and her successes, just as it points out those of Blair and Cameron/Clegg. We British have an intuitive grasp of the warp and weft of life – and perhaps a limited expectation of success and transformation. We are willing to see progress made and lost and regained, as we see the tides pushing the waves up a pebbly beach and taking them down again. It is noisy, sometimes spectacular, but always ultimately futile. Enoch Powell's famous dictum that all political careers end in failure is truer in Britain than it is in the United States. Powell's dictum was a flattening one; it reminds us that we are all – even the grandest of us – heading for the same destination. In America, some careers actually end in success – think Reagan or Roosevelt – and the overriding view is that they have been, on balance, a triumph. So when you talk failure in American politics you do not necessarily accept the Powell view that you are not talking about anything unusual. To fail in America, in politics or in any other area of life, is really to fail. The excuse that Powell provides – everyone fails – is not available to you. The second act, in which everyone and everything is levelled, is not played in the American theatre.

Which leaves us wondering about how America will cope with the relative decline of her prestige and power that the next few decades will surely bring. American energy is devoted to winning, not taking part. It is going to be frustrating when other nations, and potentially other political systems, seem to be getting ahead, leading the world, setting the bar. The big question – and here is where we are so utterly different from them – is that of co-operation and pooled sovereignty. We are used to it. Britain, in the post-Falklands world, is more or less relaxed with the idea that if we do big things in the future we will do them with others. Our aircraft carriers, literally and metaphorically, have no jets to fly off them. In our dealings with everyone, friend and foe, there will be an element of compromise. To be sure, we may have something to say and we may expect to get our way but it will be in cahoots with others. America is not there. Americans – most Americans – seriously believe that the founding fathers gave them the gift not just of constitutional independence but also of permanent freedom to act in accordance with the desires of the nation, irrespective of the opinions of lesser folks with lesser political systems. Nothing exemplifies this better than the fact that Americans are incredibly difficult to pin down when it comes to international treaties. American presidents often sign them but the Senate, whose job it is to ratify them and pass them into American law, quite frequently simply refuses. From the League of Nations to the International Criminal Court, America has a tradition of standing alone.

Many friends of America wonder why this nation, whose fundamental judgements are often perfectly in line with those of reasonable people elsewhere, cannot bring itself to take part in world society, to *play nice*, as the Americans teach their children. After all, many of the institutions of the modern world were set up by America. The UN is in New York, not Beijing.

But this is where the differing psychologies – ours and theirs – can be instructive. You have to look at what the British have internalised in the way of angst and failure and struggle. Or what the Americans have not had to cope with. They are not made like us. Their house is not falling down. They are still building, they want to think. The sun is still rising, they want to think. Tomorrow should be better than today, they want to think. To expect a people who want to believe these things, who have them at the core of their beings, to be cool about decline is to be unrealistic at best. The Wikileaks controversy of 2010 demonstrated the difficulties the Americans are having in coming to terms with the new world order. On the one hand, Hillary Clinton's State Department was determined to keep ahead of the pack and believed that it had a right to do so; the instruction revealed by Wikileaks that American diplomats should steal biometric data from senior UN staff is evidence of a mindset that

is, to put it mildly, interestingly old-fashioned in its
pursuit of national self-interest. And yet, at the same
time, Wikileaks revealed American behaviour that was
perfectly, indeed naively, collegiate and mindful and
respectful of the new order. In Yemen, for instance,
the pretence that the local government was attacking
terrorists (when in fact it was American missiles) was
sensitively, and probably sensibly, arranged by General
Petraeus, then head of local US forces. America did not
rush in like a bull in a china shop. America thought
about what to do; consulted as well. The entire picture
to emerge from the Wikileaks dump hardly suggests
that the Americans are out of control; in fact, rather
the opposite.

Then in 2011 came Egypt and Libya and the rest.
And for America, a D-Day of sorts. An opportunity to
storm some new beaches and – stretching the analogy
a bit, but only a bit – having helped to win the peace,
to secure a role in managing the post-war reality. After
the Second World War it was known as the Truman
Doctrine: President Truman vowed to fight to keep
Greece and Turkey, and, later, all of Western Europe
free of communism and he did it by fair means and
foul, with money and friendship and the occasional
dirty trick to keep legitimate Communist parties in
Italy and elsewhere on the hop. And so it might prove

to be with America and Islamist forces in the modern Middle East. Except that America's desire to storm the beaches in 2011 has been pretty negligible. Its zest for the fight has deserted it, even though zest for fights is one of the things that – as I point out elsewhere – defines America. The weakest part of Barack Obama's speech in Westminster Hall in 2011 was the section that dealt with the Arab uprisings. It seemed to suggest some kind of ownership of them but didn't really back this claim up with practical promises of real help. This, then, is not a happy situation.

At a vital moment during the tense negotiations that led up to the UN Security Council resolution on Libya, a friend of mine who is a senior US diplomat received a text on his secure office phone. Excusing himself from the table, he found a place where he could not be over-looked and brought the message onto the screen.

"We need more rinse aid," it said.

It was his wife hoping he might be able to concentrate on two things at once.

The pressure she exerted on her husband is directly analogous to the pressures on the modern American world-view. Can you sort out the rinse aid at the same time as sorting out the world? Does the rinse aid get bought if money and time and effort are being spent in places where they don't even have dishwashers?

Should you make sure the rinse aid is bought even at the expense of your other priorities?

Set aside for a minute the fact that President Obama was in charge as the Middle East burst into political life – the challenge was not just for him and the response was also a wider affair. This was about America and its view of its place in the world. The indispensable nation – as a former secretary of state called it – looked on from the sidelines as the Egypt crisis unfolded. At first America denied that President Mubarak was in trouble. Then they decided he was and needed to go. In Libya they decided that military action was "loose talk" and then engaged in it anyway a week or two later – then pulled away and let other nations get on with it. None of this looked very joined up. Critics of President Obama admonished him personally for this indecision, if that is what it was. But perhaps the blame needs to rest with the whole nation. Americans themselves were utterly torn over the whole Arab uprising. Not just torn between left and right, or interventionists versus non-interventionists, but torn inside their minds as well; struggling to work out whether America's interest in cheap oil trumped her interest in freedom, whether supporting democracy in the Middle East might lead to longer-term threats to democracy in the West. But above all, America was unsure about what its role should be in a world in which a changed relationship between Washington and every other capital was a given. Does it make sense in the second decade of this century to do things that upset the Brazilians (who abstained on the UN Security Council resolution authorising the Libya action)? The question would have sounded ludicrous a few years ago, but now, in the age of relative decline, the age of the rise of new powers, it does not seem so silly.

So what should America do? The polls showed no great thrust of opinion one way or the other. The prominent Republican Newt Gingrich even managed to argue both ways with equal vehemence – that America should get stuck in on the side of freedom, and then that the fighting in Libya was a travesty because the US had no vital interests in the region. One well-known Washington intellectual told me at the time that Barack Obama had promised change but actually delivered the foreign policy of Brent Scowcroft, the famously unsentimental and realistic National Security Adviser of the first President Bush. He did not mean this as a compliment, but many Americans might have agreed with a shrug of the shoulders; America, in other words, was embracing a new reality, a new normal, in which the nation, by choice, would look to a tradition that has always been represented in its top echelons – the tradition of caution and even isolationism in foreign affairs – and accentuate that tradition by giving it a new and central post-war importance.

The painfulness of this debate was obvious for all to see at the beginning of 2011. Barack Obama maintained his customary cool – even going on a visit to South America while US forces were first in action over Libya – but the nation fretted about whether it was doing too little or too much. The French and (it was claimed) the Qataris led the way – propelled into world leadership roles by America's unwillingness to take the position that its people have become used to adopting. The French? Really? Almost nobody in America could place Qatar on a map. Why were they leading this operation? Who were they?

As the CNN political analyst Gloria Borgia put it:

> When the President says… "We should not be afraid to act – but the burden of action should not be America's alone," we get it. But we also start wondering: What happens if we're not driving the car? We always drive the car. Truth is, we like to drive. And when we're not driving, we think it's easy – even likely – for the coalition to veer off course. So here's the conundrum: we don't want to go it alone. Yet we're not sure we trust others to take the lead.

As the sand continues to swirl around the Middle East, it is too easy to see America's discomfort and apparent diffidence at key moments as being a function of the Obama presidency. It is undoubtedly the case that this President is more open to rumination than many previous occupants of the Oval Office – he promised as much when he campaigned and he has been as good as his word. But to suggest that it is all about Obama is to miss, perhaps, a key moment in modern history. America has reached a point where the urge to drive the car, the urge to lead, has run up against the reality of a new world order in which other nations are on the rise, and in which America itself feels unsettled and unconfident about its domestic affairs. It is worth pointing out that Washington – for all the talk of decline – was able to get the Libya action going while still heavily committed in Afghanistan. The military might of America – the cruise missiles and the planes and the sheer logistical majesty of its massive military machine – was still very much on show in Libya at the start of the operation; indeed, one wonders whether it really could have happened at all without the Americans being there, and ready to press the start button.

But having said that, the picture that emerges politically from recent events is of a giant rethinking of America's behaviour. This rethink – which is not yet over and must encompass at least one change of presidency to become anything like permanent – affects America's relationship with the whole of the outside world, but more importantly, it affects its relationship with itself – the understanding that Americans have of who they are. My sense is that hesitancy over Libya, diffidence and dithering in foreign affairs, comes not from the difficulties encountered around the world but more profoundly from a sense that all is not well at home. Americans, like Britons, are having to come to terms with the long-term aftermath of an economic calamity and a consequent loss of power.

However their depression in the face of decline is far more intense that ours. Part of this is psychological: they are not used to being in this place. But part of it too is brought on by a horrible realisation that they might be even worse off than the Europeans because they do not have a governing structure capable of dealing with the needs of the times. American government is in serious trouble and is troubled by that trouble, as the journalist Mort Zuckerman put it:

> We still possess the most appealing popular culture and public values, as well as the most innovative and competent business culture. American exceptionalism endures. But we must confront our dysfunctional and profligate

government. America was founded on the principle of creating a better life for our children and grandchildren. We can do it. We aren't doing it.

In an article for *US News and World Report*, written shortly after the midterm elections of 2010, Zuckerman phrased it like this:

> The supreme confidence, national pride, and sense of achievement that marked the nation through its first 200 years have been transformed into a mood of doubt…
>
> Even the wealthiest and most highly educated are anxious at the decline of America's competitiveness. We seem unable to produce new generations of qualified leaders in the fields of science and technology. Our government has been incapable of addressing the nation's problems rationally and constructively. We are haunted that the world is catching up with America; the sense of uniqueness and self-esteem that has been a part of our national character since our founding – and has been amplified since World War II – is steadily eroding.

But the psychology of the place is still different and still out of line with our British post-imperial approach to world affairs. The reckless energy is still there at the heart of the American world mission. Can we help them cope with it? Run it off, perhaps, as you do with a toddler? This approach is doomed, as is every other effort at patronising the Americans. There has to be a better way; a way that grasps the essence of America and works with it, respects it, allows it the space it needs to live and breathe.

Americans, to be fully functioning, must be optimistic. Sometimes we forget how important it is to their peace of mind. Take the Heroic Imagination Project at Stanford University. Its website informs us:

> It's true. The world is indeed a dangerous place, and inhumane behavior – whether extraordinary evil or an individual act of cruelty – is unfortunately pervasive. But it is often entirely avoidable if only we trust ourselves to speak up, to call attention, to act responsibly. Why, then, is it so very difficult for the vast majority of us to take action in a crisis? What leaves so many people silent and paralyzed in the face of injustice or physical peril? Is heroic behavior a rare exception to the norms of human nature? We at the Heroic Imagination Project believe the answer is absolutely not. We believe heroism can be learned by example and reinforced with practice. Our programs are designed to inspire heroism in ordinary people and teach them to make wise and effective decisions when heroic opportunities arise.

The *Today* programme arranged an interview with the boss of the project, a psychologist of some repute, but eventually we decided that the piece was unusable. It was not exactly the content, which was interesting enough. It was not the arguments and ideas or the accent that made us drop it: it was just that, well, the whole thing seemed so, umm, American! Culturally, we decided, it simply could not run; it would be regarded by the *Today* audience as utter gobbledygook. It was not a case of potentially broadening minds or introducing foreign and difficult concepts. No: this was a category error, as the philosophers put it; where the two parts of the equation (the *Today* audience and the Heroic Imagination Project) simply could not meet because they were so utterly, profoundly, logically (ontologically!) separate. The idea of teaching heroism is not going to take off in Britain. In America it would be universally accepted: *way to go!*

This is why it hurts Americans when people are not heroic. Ronald Reagan, in his first inaugural speech, referred to America as "a living, breathing presence, unimpressed by what others say is impossible, proud of its own success; generous, yes, and naive; sometimes wrong, never mean, always impatient to provide a better life for its people in a framework of a basic fairness and freedom". I still recognise his America – viewed, perhaps, with the generosity of an affectionate outsider – but many Americans frankly do not. They still want to think in these terms, but faced with the evidence, they find it difficult.

What does the future hold for them and how can we help, or hinder, the process of America's coming to terms with the modern world? It is worth being honest with ourselves first on the subject of debt. It is a fact that America's greatness (and Britain's) was created by debt, or a willingness to use debt as a tool, allied to prudence about finding ways of paying back that debt in the long term. Without debt the English-speaking peoples would be much diminished as forces in world history. In *God and Gold,* Walter Russell Mead points out that the century that really created the modern dominance of the US – the nineteenth century – saw America having to borrow money in every year: "The American nation was a debtor nation throughout the nineteenth century; it was a much greater and richer country after one hundred years of debt." The same was the case – as every economic historian would accept – for Britain in the key periods of our history when our power was being entrenched: we borrowed, paid it back and borrowed some more.

So what is the fuss about? There are two reasons why modern American government debt – the cumulative total of each year's difference between what is spent and what is raised in taxes – is such a massive threat. The first is that the actual sums – as a percentage of national wealth – are very high. Within a few years America is likely to owe roughly the same as it is worth. In Britain the figure that so spooked the incoming coalition government in 2010 was that our debt had reached around 60 per cent of our wealth. So America's debt is very high. It has been high before – around the time of the Second World War – but not nearly as high in any peacetime period. The second reason why American debt might be so catastrophic in the modern era is that the baby boomers are retiring and are about to put unprecedented strain on the system of benefits – medical and social – that is aimed at older Americans. These payments to these people have been guaranteed and must be made. So if the Chinese decide to lend less to America and the dollar interest rate rises, America faces a period of potentially catastrophic austerity. Even if the Chinese stay friendly, it has been suggested that by 2025 America will raise only enough in taxes to cover entitlement spending (unemployment benefits, health spending for the elderly and disabled, pensions etc) and interest payments; everything else, from defence to transport to security to energy to education, will have to be borrowed money.

This America, the America described by the facts just mentioned, is a very different place to the jolly(ish) nation we think of today. The potential for domestic strife is huge as is the potential for complete withdrawal from the outside world. Getting on for a quarter of US debt is held by the Chinese government. What if China, facing its own domestic pressures, decides to go rogue and slash its dollar holdings? What if China simply pulls the rug from under the US? As one commentator has put it, with reference to America's continuing defence of Taiwan from a Chinese takeover: "Chinese central bankers could prove more dangerous than Chinese Admirals." In other words, the threat of economic disaster could well persuade the Americans to ditch allies and ditch commitments. And it is not just the Chinese. Who will listen to the US if they know that the nation is in crisis and cannot afford to pay its way? American power will be reduced in practical reality and their example – the shining city on the hill – will also be tarnished since the system the Americans have long told us is the best turns out to have ruined them.

But it is not just the debt. It is the failure to be able to deal with it. Here the UK shows the way and the Americans are left flailing in our wake. Let me be very clear here: I am not talking about the actual policy adopted by the coalition government. I am not suggesting that they were right or they were wrong to go down the road they chose. Nor am I suggesting that Barack Obama was right or wrong to take the actions he took in the first few years of his presidency. My point is a deeper one: in Britain we were still capable of taking those decisions. Our political system was flexible enough and open enough for a reasonably honest debate (at least post-election) of what our options might be and what courses of action were available.

No such debate is possible in America. One of the great features of modern American life is the utter debasement of their politics. People focus on the language used and the recklessness of the arguments – and in Chapter Nine I explore the possible reasons for this and whether British broadcasting rules might be part of the reason we escape such nastiness – but the really fundamental problem is not the roughness of the language or the craziness of the tobacco-chewing cousin-marrying folks: it is the inability of Americans, including clever, well-educated, sophisticated Americans, to engage in a real debate about what options their nation has.

An example is Sarah Palin's home state, Alaska. When I say Alaska, what comes to mind? Snow probably.

Frozen wastes. Animals. Hunting. Rugged stuff and rugged folks – millions of miles from Washington and millions of miles from the cosseted lives of Americans who live in the suburbs of the big cities. Wrong. As the commentator Anne Applebaum put it:

> The hypocrisy at the heart of the [Republican] party – and at the heart of American politics – is at its starkest in Alaska. For decades, Alaskans have lived off federal welfare. Taxpayers' money subsidizes everything from Alaska's roads and bridges to its myriad programs for Native Americans. Federal funding accounts for one-third of Alaskan jobs. Nevertheless, Alaskans love to think of themselves as the last frontiersmen, the inhabitants of a land "beyond the horizon of urban clutter," a state with no use for Washington and its wicked ways.

The unreality exists too in the realm of guns. I have written before about how peaceful America often seems as a place to live; although it has more murders than other civilised nations, it has less minor crime. I do not think that taking America's guns from their owners (not a realistic proposition anyway) would necessarily make the nation better. It would save some lives for sure; but guns are too tightly woven into the fabric of American life for their non-existence to be contemplated. However, there is a complete fallacy at the heart of what many Americans believe about guns and this fallacy is part of the depressing myopia that poisons American political debate. The fallacy is this: that guns are what guarantee American freedom: of religion, of conscience, of daily life. The truth is that if you look around the world at societies that are gun-infested or gun-protected (take your pick), there is quite obviously no link between personal possession of weapons and freedom. As *The Economist* put it, with admirable clarity and coolness, shortly after the infamous attack on a congresswoman in Arizona in 2010 in which a number of people, including a nine-year-old child, died:

> There is no link between individual ownership of firearms and democratic governance or civil rights and freedoms. The main determinant of guns per population member, as for cars per population member, is wealth. And yet, while the United States has the most guns per person in the world, the number two country appears to be Yemen, not usually considered a bastion of democracy or civil rights. Individual ownership of firearms is much higher in Saudi Arabia and Russia than in Britain; it is much higher in Pakistan than in India. The idea that individuals could use their private firearms to mount a serious challenge to government hegemony is only plausible in very weak states. When individuals, militia or criminal gangs foolishly attempt to directly challenge police or the National Guard in

the United States, they are quickly overpowered, killed or arrested.

It's an important point, this. During my time in America I always felt that the British obsession with American gun crime was overblown – guns are part of America and most gun owners are decent peaceful people. But here is an uncomfortable fact. My old house at 3805 Windom Place has the zip code 20016, and I've discovered that since the Supreme Court relaxed gun ownership laws in Washington, one zip code above all others has accounted for a surge in gun-buying: 20016. This feels to me like a kind of madness. When I called on the neighbours recently, I pushed open their front door – they would not have thought to lock it. 20016 is one of the safest places to live *in the world*. Sometimes someone parks a car facing the wrong way – you are meant to park facing the direction of traffic – but this is the limit of local criminality. Nobody who has bought a gun in 20016 can possibly have done it out of a rational belief that he or she was reducing the risk of being attacked. So why did they? The reason is deeper and it seems to me – with my newfound detachment from American life – worrying. Americans have long convinced themselves of the falsehood that *The Economist* so tellingly debunks: that there is a link between guns and freedom at the level of society; that the more guns there are in the hands of individuals, the more difficult it would be for a dictator to take power. This is the freedom guaranteed by the second amendment to the constitution passed in 1791. And still the argument about gun control is an argument about what the amendment actually means. It is the wrong argument! The real argument should be whether civilised societies in the modern age are made safer by guns – but that argument is beyond America. So far beyond America that even Barack Obama, who cannot really be a friend of guns, has done precisely nothing to advance the agenda of those who would limit gun ownership. The debate on gun ownership in the US is skewed by the failure of those opposed to guns to state clearly and honestly the obvious truth: guns do not guarantee liberty in modern America. There may be all manner of reasons for keeping them but that really should not be one of them. It is a way of thinking similar to the Alaskans and their potty self-image as frontiersmen even while they suck at the teat of central government. But nobody in modern America can tell the Alaskans not to be so silly and nobody tells the National Rifle Association that either.

Barack Obama is as guilty here as any other politician. When gun ownership in Washington DC was an issue before the Supreme Court in 2008 (with the court being lobbied to allow greater gun rights), he kept quiet. He had little other choice. Because of the utterly false link in many American minds between guns and freedom, he would have been committing electoral suicide to speak out. He wanted to win in states where Democrats had as many guns as anyone else – states like Montana, where the Democratic Party Governor told me in no uncertain terms that he would never back any kind of limit on weapons: "For us, gun control is hitting what you shoot at!"

The point is vitally important to an understanding of modern American politics and the modern American crisis. Americans have seriously lost touch with reality. Alaskans are not the only folks to have kidded themselves that they are living lives which, in reality, they are not. The whole nation has rendered itself incapable of holding a proper debate about what to do regarding its debt because nobody really understands – or is capable of admitting – what the problem is and what the options are. There is no better example than tax. Nobody likes paying taxes but part of the solution to the financial crisis of recent years has got to be a rise in government income. No serious person on either side of the Atlantic disputes this. But there are very few serious people on the US side. It is pathetic to see Americans scrabbling around trying to fund their education system through sponsorship from fizzy drinks manufacturers, trying to fund their mental health services through state lotteries that contribute to the breakdown and misery the money is then spent alleviating. Tax avoidance – on a national scale – has somehow become part of the American self-image. This is a historical nonsense. Throughout most of the twentieth century – the American century – national income tax levels were higher than they are now. American governments in the past have been able to raise the funds to build the nation and invest in its future. Now if you suggest a VAT for America (not a bad idea as it is a tax that can be collected easily and is difficult to avoid), you are painted as a wild-eyed socialist. Even plans to reduce the current 100-per-cent tax exemption for mortgage interest payments (100 per cent!) are hugely controversial. Americans – taking a leaf out of their Alaskan neighbours' book – simply refuse to grasp that they are massive consumers of government funds and they need to find the money from somewhere. True, there are some Americans who genuinely and intellectually coherently argue for a smaller state, but they are nowhere near a majority. Most Americans in the 21st century have come to see themselves as frontiersmen but they want to live the lives (particularly when they retire) of French civil servants. Dissonance is the mildest way of describing it. Utter barminess comes closer. And it infects all aspects of the debate on the choices available – because nobody is being really honest about what kind of a nation America is.

And the dishonesty allows both main political parties to avoid the tough choices they are forever talking about taking. This is how the economist Jeffrey Sachs sees it:

> The problem is America's corrupted politics and loss of civic morality. One political party, the Republicans, stands for little except tax cuts, which they place above any other goal. The Democrats have a bit wider set of interests, including support for healthcare, education, training, and infrastructure. But, like the Republicans, the Democrats, too, are keen to shower tax cuts on their major campaign contributors, predominantly rich Americans. The result is a dangerous paradox. The US budget deficit is enormous and unsustainable. The poor are squeezed by cuts in social programmes and a weak job market. One in eight Americans depends on food stamps to eat. Yet, despite these circumstances, one political party wants to gut tax revenues altogether, and the other is easily dragged along, against its better

instincts, out of concern for keeping its rich contributors happy.

Where do we come in? It seems to me that the debate about military approaches to world problems versus softer power needs to be upgraded and made more concrete. Britain needs to encourage America to be more honest about the kinds of economic choices available in the coming years and the kinds of implications they have for the world. British politicians need to encourage the Americans to understand that they can maintain their central position in the affairs of the planet *only* if they sort out their economy, and that has to start with sorting out their politics, regaining the ability to make choices, an ability vital to a proper functioning democracy.

They have to have a better understanding of their own history. Presidents Truman and Eisenhower both fought the Cold War with great vigour, yet both understood that economic strength at home was as vital as skirmishes in foreign lands. They improved science education and built highways. Today, that means concentrating on sorting out Mexico rather than Afghanistan or Libya, on addressing illegal immigration and boosting trade. It does not mean withdrawal from the outside world nor an end to involvement in foreign wars, but it does mean recognising that America's key contribution to the world is the example of its domestic self. Americans need to get away from their foolish obsession with the language of their constitution and even with some of its certainties. Samuel Huntington once referred to America as a "Tudor Polity": he meant that the patterns of government Americans prefer – decentralised and in constant opposition – are in fact modelled on sixteenth-century Britain, where power was diffuse and held by the Church, the Inns of Court, the barons and the municipal corporations as much as by the Tudor monarchs. Guys, seriously, this may not be the best way of approaching the new century! Perhaps our politicians need to be more honest in telling Americans that they have to pull their socks up. It need not be a hectoring message or a condescending one; in fact it is the opposite of condescending since it recognises the indispensability of the world's richest nation. It is a message from a true ally – no longer wittering on foolishly about the nature of our relationship, but using our linguistic and cultural closeness to some real purpose.

Chapter Six

AUTUMN HAS PROVED the strangest, most discombobulating time of year for a family settling back into English life. By the time our second autumn came along, we were beginning to feel confident once again with the hallmarks of Englishness: the price of petrol, the sense of irony, the mists and mellow fruitfulness. All was going swimmingly. Until we were knocked off balance by the trees.

Fall colours – colors to be accurate – are one of the great joys of American life. You do not get them anywhere else. This is the American conceit and we believed it with the passion of all immigrants to the New World. As the United States National Arboretum website has it: "In areas that are often cloudy for much of the autumn, with rather warm temperatures, fall colors are dull at best. This is often the case in much of Europe."

Ouch. That puts us in our place. The ideal conditions for brilliant autumn colours are a warm, wet spring combined with a sunny, cool autumn. We often have the former on our side of the pond but the Americans are right: we rarely enjoy the latter. Americans have these conditions – especially in New England but also extending down south into Virginia – almost every year. The result is breathtaking; in particular, I always felt, when savoured alongside that other great American vista: the sleazy glamour of the road I mentioned in the introduction, the glamour that both repels and appeals to visitors – and indeed Americans themselves – in roughly equal measure.

America, as you know, can be pretty ugly. The tat! And then turn a corner and your jaw will drop. A panorama of the mundane gives way to America's greatest asset: its space and its natural beauty.

The colours of the American autumn, the coppers, the yellows, the deep reds and purples, stretch in some states for as far as the eye can see. America has always, right from the beginning, been a land of trees. The American historian James Harmon McElroy suggested that the taming of the forest and the wilderness has been the principal event in the history of the American people; everything else has flowed from this struggle to preserve nature but to conquer it as well.

Now this is where our autumn colours come in. In 2010, without doubt, we challenged the good folk of the United States to rethink their view of the dank European fall. Walking on the hills outside Bath, we were shocked as a family to see sights that we thought we had left behind for ever. A genuine New England vista in old England. The whole marvellous copper-tinged, yellow-flecked gorgeousness laid out before us, with the city of Bath thrown in for good measure.

It was a surprise, this view, and that, it occurred to us later, was itself an added bonus. Because one of the great ironies of American life is that along with the space and the freedom and the sense of rugged adventure that living there can bring – the fact that American woods really do have bears in them and American weather can kill with its hurricanes and tornadoes and apocalyptic electrical storms – there is also in the American psyche a desire, as James Harmon McElroy suggests, to tame all of this wildness.

So the American fall colours are often experienced in a dispiritingly regimented way. The trip from Washington DC to the absolutely stunning Skyline Drive is a case in point. This road runs for a hundred miles along the crest of the Blue Ridge Mountains in Shenandoah National Park. It is breathtaking because the crest really is a crest: the hills fall away and the vistas on both sides are huge and unspoiled. But it's gated! You cannot get onto the road without going past a little lodge and paying a toll. And once you've paid and are on the road, there is no stopping except at designated vista points. There is no walking unless you keep to the paths, and each one has been thoughtfully graded for you in advance so that you can judge whether Granny or the kids will survive this brush with nature.

In other parts of the country, there are entire websites devoted to telling you which autumnal colour will be where and for how long. They have turned autumn into an industry. It is the American way.

So we should doubly celebrate our English autumns when they burst into life and shock us all. First, because they provide an explosion of colour and a reminder that even in our crowded nation, with its mild and uninteresting weather, we can manage beauty that competes with anywhere else on earth. But the real joy is the surprise. The Americans can boast of how dependable their fall can be but its very dependability dulls the colour, as it were; real vibrancy is unforced, unexpected, untrammelled by rules and regulations and guides to the best views and the gentlest paths. Life in England is more colourful than I remembered. More than ever, after that walk near Bath, I was glad to be back.

And yet when you try to put your finger on quite why this might be, the task is oddly difficult. What are the psychological drivers of America's desire to impose order? Does it really all come from the challenge of those vast forests that greeted the first settlers? Is there an atavistic need to fight off bears that makes Americans as they are? And the same questions can be asked of the British: why are we so bloody relaxed about everything? Why do we stumble upon autumn colours and have no need to be told where to go and what to do?

To my semi-outsider's eyes, the Britishness of the British was revealed most markedly in the fallout from the years of New Labour in one particular area of national life. In a desire to organise Cool Britannia into a functioning security-dominated theme park – a very American view of society that lay at the heart of much of what Tony Blair, and to an extent Gordon Brown, wanted to do – they lost sight of the great unwillingness of the British to be organised, dragooned.

So here is another area in which we can help the Americans to refind their better selves and in doing so to refind the kind of mental capacity that led to the successes of their past. We have to help them with their failure to see the wood for the trees. For they have become so sclerotic in their habits that they have lost the flexibility to act in their own best interest: inventing Google but falling behind in maths education; inventing Google but failing to notice that the world is networked and traditional power structures outdated; inventing Google but not noticing that they invented Google.

The real issue here is whether America can be persuaded to do what is necessary to continue to lead in a changed world. Americans need to be persuaded that they have the capacity and the social structure that could render all the talk of Chinese and Indian dominance premature, if not utterly redundant. I think it can be done. And it begins with demographics. America is small and young. We are not used to seeing it in those terms but it is the truth. Its population burst through 300 million – to much celebration – in 2006 and will get to 400 million in the next few decades, but these numbers are modest and manageable when set against the actual and potential populations of India and China. Those nations have to cope with territorial and ethnic divisions and political structures that take note of those divisions without allowing them to become dominant drivers in local politics. America does not have these problems. There is nothing fissiparous about the US (alright, the Alaskans have muttered about independence but they are, as we have already seen, deluded) and there is a cultural myth to which most Americans subscribe. *Ça marche!* Will China? Will India?

I was struck by the sight of the Chinese Olympics' opening ceremony. In so many respects the games were a showcase for the new Asian century. They were spectacular and well organised and stunning. And yet when you looked at the opening ceremony – the parade of teams through the main hall – the weakness of so much of the world was also on show. All those athletes who looked so completely as you expected them to. The Italians, the Congolese, the Russians and, of course, more than anything, the Indians and the Chinese. They were ethnically and socially similar; representing nations nervous about interconnectivity. Then in came the Americans. Madness! A great seething mass of humanity with every look and every background on show. Americans from Africa, Americans from Asia, Americans from Europe, Americans from the Middle East, Americans from Mars and Venus and all points in between. Throughout history, this ability to attract talent and cope with influxes of humanity has been part of the American way, but now there is a special relevance to it.

This century is the century of the network. It is the Wikicentury. Terrorists use them and governments use them but so do universities and societies and companies and individuals. The nation state has not withered away but it has been overtaken in many important ways by those who can connect with each other, share ideas and share experiences, innovate and re-create in an atmosphere of genuine freedom, a culture that respects troublesome views as much as it respects conformity. America used to be good at this and could be good at it again. You can have any number of science parks – Chinese style – but if you do not have the freedom to chat on the internet about what you are discovering and what implications it might have, you miss out on the real driving force of the future: being at the hub of the network. To be there requires a culture, political and social, that values people who speak their mind. It also needs to value truth as best we know it – scientific truth, which is always open to challenge. This is why America's broadcasting set-up, I believe, needs to take a long, hard look at whether it encourages shouting at the expense of anything like proper freedom for competing ideas to be understood and evaluated. America can learn from us in this and we need to be ready to spell it out: freedom should allow unpopular or even eccentric ideas to be heard. Drowning out dissent is for the Chinese and for Fox News.

There is a wonderful book by Robert Wright called *Non Zero: the Logic of Human Destiny*. It was published before 9/11, so became a bit crowded out by military matters and the struggle for the immediate future of human destiny. But in the longer term the ideas in this book need to be looked at again. Wright suggests that history is – contrary to the fashion these days – a story of the evolution and improvement of humankind. The fundamental improvement is the realisation that life need not be zero-sum: in other words, my gain need not be your loss. We can both gain, from trade, from friendship, from the sharing of art. The biggest benefits, if Wright is right, will accrue to those nations who can be in a position to gain in the future because they are in the centre of the hub, open culturally, physically and mentally to all that everyone has to say.

This is not an argument that the internet solves everything. The net can be used by authoritarian powers and can be a tool of social control. But if a nation can position itself as genuinely open to ideas and genuinely chatty in the connected world, then it has a mighty advantage.

It is really about creative tension and creative energy. It is about using information as power on a truly global stage. It is about government power to act quickly because the kind of information that used to be provided – unreliably – by spies and satellites is increasingly going to be there for the taking if only you have the eyes to see and the linguistic and intellectual skills to use the knowledge when it comes. It is about the power of commercial interests to seize opportunities before competitors even know the opportunities are there. It is about the power of individuals to cross borders without passports. Will all this happen in China and India? Could it?

The point is that America is in a position to achieve continuing power and influence (authority is perhaps the better word) through giving up on hegemony. We have to help them by persuading ourselves that power in the future will not come through the kind of dominance represented by all those US military bases that dot the globe. In fact, most of them can close. Power will come from an understanding that human diversity is to be celebrated and ideas and divergences of opinion and solutions that begin as eccentric and eventually become mainstream must all be encouraged. The poor old European Union, top down in structure and thinking, can be left in the dust by an America that celebrates the triumph of the small and inconvenient and unorthodox.

The problem for American is getting there. The temptations not to – to focus on old allies (London and Washington or Paris and Washington) – are real and ever present. But the prize for all of us if America breaks free is incalculable: a world in which the dominant force is progressive and humane, focused on medical advance rather than religious conformity, on problem-solving rather than blame-fixing; that is the true prize.

America has to be persuaded to go back to the forests and the fall colours and just let them be. It has to go back to being surprised and energised. It has to abandon its gated communities. It has to maintain an immigration policy that encourages entry wherever possible. It has, in particular, to focus (and we should be telling them this and in doing so willingly kissing goodbye to the "bust of Churchill" idiocy) on the South American nations and the potential that they have in the future to build a powerbase of trade and innovation. If Mexico was rich and stable, how much better off would all Americans be? If Brazil were to be a serious diplomatic ally, for instance on Libya, how much more powerful would American ideas be in the future, than if America looks to London for the kind of unquestioning but resentful and half-hearted support it's all too often had in the past? Should America move to kick Britain off the UN Security Council? In public, this is not for serious consideration; in private, the thought is there and the reason – realistic appraisal of the future benefits that might accrue to the world

– might not be antithetical to British interests. We have to allow them to get there.

We should set the Yanks free. They'll do themselves – and in the process, us – a power of good.

Chapter Seven

Amid fields of clover,
T'was just a little over a hundred years ago,
A handful of strangers, they faced many dangers,
to make their country grow.
It's now quite a nation of wond'rous population,
And free from ev'ry king!
It's your land, it's my land,
A great do or die land,
And that's just why I sing:

America, I love you!
You're like a sweetheart of mine!
From ocean to ocean,
For you my devotion, is touching each bound'ry line.
Just like a little baby
Climbing its mother's knee,
America, I love you!
And there's a hundred million others like me!
American patriotic song, 1915

FREE FROM EV'RY KING! The line reminds us that there are days when we diverge. One such was November 16th, 2010, the day on which two significant pieces of British national news were announced. The first was already a talking point by morning: an expected acknowledgement by the government that it had made the decision to pay out money – quite large sums – to a number of individuals who said they had been tortured by the Americans and others in the war on terror, with the knowledge of the UK security services. It was an extraordinary moment. The government made the case that the cost of defending itself against the claims made by the men concerned would be too huge to bear. The outcome of the case was too uncertain to risk. How odd, some sniffed, from the nation that brought us Agincourt and the Charge of the Light Brigade, and Dunkirk and D-Day. Cost too great. Uncertainty of outcome too much. Best pack it in and get on with something else.

And, as if by magic, something else came along. A royal wedding, plucked from the pages of a fairy tale, so gorgeous and magical that it had David Cameron's cabinet members banging the table with delight. You didn't have to be American to find all this a little, umm, weird. But it helped. One amazed American news magazine correspondent wrote that the day had started with news of the torture payout, "but as I write BBC News 24 is burbling on ad nauseam about what a modern couple the royal lovebirds are, about what kind of dress 'Princess Catherine' should choose, about where the wedding will take place. A helicopter circles above Buckingham Palace".

The writer went on to acknowledge that plenty of Americans would be fascinated by the royal wedding (isn't that one good reason why we have them?) but their fascination is too easily confused with admiration. When the wedding day arrived, there was, of course, huge American interest. The networks sent their top people and the audiences in the US were respectable. The Duke and Duchess of Cambridge made Canada and the US their first destination for an official visit. But: it always struck me, living in America, that that line in the ever-popular ditty, "and free from ev'ry king", carries a punch that we subjects of Her Majesty fail fully to grasp. Several US newspapers, on the announcement of the wedding, delved into the English class system with great gusto and reported the oddities of how dukes and earls became dukes and earls. What fun they had with the word "commoner". How thrilled they would have been to hear the BBC royal correspondent informing listeners to Radio Four that the new princess was "middle class". How would he have known? If you are British you know how he knows. If you are American, and knew that her mum and dad were self-made millionaires, you would be mystified. And not just mystified. Frustrated, too, by a nation whose population seriously believes that it is divided into royals, nobles, and commoners, and that this division matters, and is immutable. As the *Wall Street Journal* commentator and former Reagan speechwriter Peggy Noonan put it: "Kate should take her polite and striving middle-class upbringing and use it to add dignity and distance to the House of Windsor." Dignity and substance, for Americans, come from what you do with your life, not where you were born. In this respect, they have much more in common with other inhabitants of republics than they do with us. They are too polite to say this to our faces but they regard the monarchy as silly and damaging to our self-worth. Fascinating, glamorous, but silly.

It is true that the pageant of our royal family is of interest to American tourists but it does not follow that deep down it leads to respect, from them, for us. When I lived in Washington I found there was a deep-seated and cross-party contempt for the trappings of royalty. One of the more gossipy revelations in the Wikileaks dump of American diplomatic telegrams in 2010 was that Prince Andrew, in his role as a backer of British trade, had been rude and uncouth at a lunch in Kyrgyzstan. Tatiana Gfoeller, Washington's Ambassador to this corrupt and repressed corner of the world, recorded in a secret cable that Andrew was cocky and "verged on the rude". Andrew attacked Britain's corruption investigators in the Serious Fraud Office for what he called "idiocy". He called *Guardian* reporters investigating bribery "those (expletive) journalists ... who poke their noses everywhere." So far, relatively unsurprising; what really stood out to me was the tone of the message from the Ambassador. She regarded Andrew as an idiot plainly enough, but also as an illegitimate idiot. In another section of her message she wrote: "His mother's subjects seated around the table roared their approval... The crowd practically clapped."

The unspoken question: why? Why would anyone take the views of this unelected blowhard seriously? He was ill-informed (the Ambassador likens his view that local corruption should be sorted out locally to telling an anorexic to sort out his or her own treatment) but far worse than that, to the eyes of an American, he was without proper standing to make these comments and to hold this position in the first place.

American views on royalty have always been ambivalent but we Brits have always failed to grasp the ambivalence. Yes, they love the royal flummery and the cute princes and horses and wagons but no, they do not, deep down, admire the system that royalty, even constitutional royalty, spawns.

The first member of the royal family to visit the United States was the heir to the British throne, the great-grandson of George III, Edward Albert, Prince of Wales. It was 1860 – the colony had been free for less than a century – and antebellum America pulled out all the stops. He was feted from the Canadian border to the South. There were balls and addresses and dinners and ovations. There was a full evening dress, candle-lit march and cavalcade down Broadway. Everywhere there were crowds: reports spoke of 30,000 organised by voluntary groups in Baltimore. The crowds were reckoned to be the biggest for any event in the nation's history. Among the highlights of the trip was a meeting between the Prince and a veteran of the revolutionary war (he was 104 years old), who said he "wished to show the boy and his soldiers that he bore no anger for old times". The Governor of Pennsylvania told Albert that "we cannot follow our ancestry more than a few generations back without tracing the line to a British Red Coat". Many years later, the American literary critic Van Wyck Brooks put it like this: "America has no childhood – in America. We left our childhood in the Old World."

Notes on Them and Us

Here is Frederick Law Olmsted on an American's first visit (in the nineteenth century) to England:

> We cannot keep still, but run about with boyish excitement. We feel indeed like children that have come back to visit the paternal house, and who are rummaging about in the garret among their father's playthings, ever and anon shouting, "See what I have found! See what I have found!"

That strikes me as a cultural fantasy as much alive today as when it was written. As another contemporary wrote: "It's not sightseeing really; we feel as if we have been there in a dream before."

So they loved the Prince in 1860 and they loved Charles in 1986. According to the *Chicago Tribune* in that year, "most simply go gaga over the British, as when you saw so many squealing gala ladies stumbling out of their ball gowns trying to press the royal flesh."

But here is the ambivalence. First, it can be found loud and clear in the coda to the visit provided by local papers, who were a little less bowled over than the ball-gown-wearing ladies. A good example is found in *Vanity Fair* which produced this mock report in 1860:

> One day the Prince of Wales was passing along when

he was met by a small boy in company of several other small boys. "My gracious," said the Prince. No more striking instance of royal sagacity has come to light.

In the magazine *Littell's Living Age,* they made a wider point:

> The honours that were paid to the English Prince could only have been offered by freemen, too confident of the greatness of their own country to fear any misconstruction of the applause which was voluntarily bestowed.

The Americans were not supplicants or receivers of patronage: that is the point. And they never have been. They are free of the British (and European) history of patronage, in which the Church and later wealthy monarchs and aristocrats were the wellspring of the good life for all, in the betterment of social conditions, the progress of the sciences, and perhaps more than in any other area, in the enormous encouragement of the arts and universities. Most Americans would suggest that this patronage – the effects of which they enjoy thoroughly as tourists – has had a baleful influence on the lives and histories of the little folks in Europe. Beneficiaries of the munificence of the ruling classes become dependents, they would suggest. We are all stick men in a Lowry painting. And when the state takes over the tasks once undertaken by the monarchs and the Church and the wealthy (as with welfare or the provision of university education, at least until 2010), the habits of patronage follow the same pattern; hence, many Americans believe, even if they are too polite to say it, the slavishness of the British and other Europeans to the state and its purposes and predilections. And, of course, sitting on top of this system is the royal correspondent whispering about the social class of the woman Prince William is marrying. Some even suggested – seriously – that the royal wedding demonstrated the classlessness of modern Britain. It did no such thing for most Americans, even those who paid good money to come and witness the happy event. They flock to see us make fools of ourselves. They love it: proof that their founding fathers were right, proof that their society is superior, proof that while there may be good opportunities for tourism in royalty, there is little else to recommend it.

Misunderstanding of how Americans view the social set-up in Britain causes us to assume wrongly that they admire our public life and wish that their presidents were more than (for instance) a peanut farmer or an actor or a clothing salesman (Truman) or a community activist or even a reality TV star. But while they might occasionally complain that the choices on offer as head of state are pretty mediocre, they would really have it no other way.

Snobbery does not respect democracy. There is a relationship between social models – and the virtues and vices that oil them – and the political set-up of any country. Courtly ideas of politeness are deliberately exclusionary tools: they serve to keep hoi polloi out. Social relationships impinge on politics. This is why Americans (however bored they are by the suburbs and however depressed they are at times by the sheer ordinariness of their land), love and value civility more than they do the genteel and courtly manners of the upper-class British. One of the great works of travel literature and national criticism aimed at America in the nineteenth century was *Domestic Manners of the Americans* by Mrs Frances Trollope, mother of the novelist Anthony Trollope. The book is a joy because it says as much about Mrs Trollope and where she comes from as it does about the Americans. She complains about everything she sees but worthiest of note are the "violent intimacy" of the natives and their habit of calling each other gentlemen and ladies in spite of the fact that (to Mrs Trollope's horrified eyes) they were quite obviously nothing of the sort. There is a wonderful scene in the book in which a German duke is reported to have been badly beaten after trying to commandeer an entire stagecoach for a long journey. Mrs Trollope thinks he should have had the right to exclusivity because of his birth; the Americans do not. If they can pay, they want to get on: owning a private stagecoach, they would admire; assuming the right through birth to take up extra seats in a public vehicle, they do not. Nothing, since that incident, has changed much.

To return to November 16th, 2010: this royalty business was not the only area where our nations were on different planets that day. The royal shenanigans were set in train on the same day as the announcement of a move many Americans saw as little more than capitulation to supporters of terrorism; evidence, as they saw it, that the West was losing the battle with militant Islam by dint of failing to stand up for itself. As one American critic wrote: "To defeat the UK government, all the former Gitmo detainees and their lawyers had to do was claim they were tortured and then bury government officials in paperwork." It did not feel to many Americans as if the Brits really had any stomach for the fight. It felt on that day, November 16th, 2010, as if the nation many older Americans look to with respect and admiration had taken leave of its senses and chosen the opiate of a royal wedding over the grimmer, tougher, more challenging reality of standing up for itself in the modern world. That feeling was to return with knobs on when, months later, Osama bin Laden was shot and the Archbishop of Canterbury declared himself uncomfortable about it, as bin Laden had been unarmed at the time.

Of course, plenty of Brits would retort that none of these cases would have been brought if the United States had not behaved outrageously, recklessly, even cruelly, in the war on terror. If Americans had been a little less gung-ho, the threat of Islamist terrorism might have been combated more sensibly and more effectively and without the need for anyone to come near a court. It is a fair point. Americans' psychological make-up persuades them that to strike out in defence of liberty is always acceptable in polite society. The treatment of the terrorist threat in a proportionate and reasoned way has been difficult for Americans. Even Barack Obama's White House has accepted the need for an extra judicial side to this fight. Waterboarding ended when he came to power, but the attacking of individuals – not convicted of any offence or even necessarily planning one – gathered pace with the use of pilotless drone aircraft, causing natural friends of the Nobel Peace Prize-winner, such as the UN, to complain that this was not what he was meant to be about.

But Obama is American. I wrote in my book *Have a Nice Day* about friends of ours in Washington who began every meal with a toast: Death to Al Qaeda! Ludicrous? Deranged? Certainly over the top: but glorious, too, it struck me, in the toast's message to friends and foes (and self): we back ourselves, we believe in ourselves, we love ourselves, we have the same faith in our values (generally decent and open and humane) as our enemies have in theirs. We will fight them on the beaches. We will never surrender.

The British way is different now. Deep down, way below the level of conscious political and social choices (about government spending, about public transport, about wind farms), we and the Americans see the modern world and its threats and opportunities from profoundly different perspectives. Even though America had a president from the left and Britain a prime minister from the right, the difference in attitudes confuses the politics to a point that makes any discussion of it irrelevant, redundant. David Cameron hinted that he understood this when he made his first visit to see Barack Obama. In an article for the *Wall Street Journal,* Mr Cameron wrote:

There is a seemingly endless British preoccupation with the health of the special relationship. Its temperature is continually taken to see if it's in good shape, its pulse checked to see if it will survive. I have never understood this anxiety. The US–UK relationship is simple: it is strong because it delivers for both of us. The alliance is not sustained by our historical ties or blind loyalty. This is a partnership of choice that serves our national interests.

This was the foundation of the relationship that became essential and was celebrated during the Obama state visit of 2011. This is not your grandfather's special relationship. The Cameron approach – which will surely be followed by subsequent prime ministers of any party – is, as Cameron has it, a relationship based firmly on the notion that the two nations are chugging along on their respective journeys through time and history and just sometimes, or perhaps often, find that they are quite remarkably agreed on a particular course of action or ultimate goal and – hey presto! – they come together and get it done. Once done, they shake hands and part, half expecting to come across each other again, like people on a blind date who think *this could be the one*, but are not quite sure and fancy having a few more dates before throwing in the towel and settling down.

This was Mrs Thatcher in her pomp:

Whatever people say, the special relationship does exist, it does count and it must continue, because the United States needs friends in the lonely task of world leadership. More than any other country, Britain shares America's passionate commitment to democracy and willingness to stand and fight for it. You can cut through all the verbiage and obfuscation. It's really as simple as that.

The crucial point is this: Cameron chooses to stress comity of interests above any metaphysical what-not about shared values and deeply understood ties of kith and kin. In doing so, I think he recognises an important truth: the values are only really shared up to a point. Deep down, on days like November 16th, 2010, the values deeply diverge.

There are those who have argued powerfully that America and Britain – engines of the English-speaking world – have a very much closer fundamental connection. Walter Russell Mead, in his magisterial *God and Gold*, is the elegant leader of this pack. His book's subtitle is *Britain, America and the making of the Modern World* and its central argument is that the extraordinary dominance of the English-speaking peoples is down, to a large extent, to the inner strength of some core beliefs that they have always shared, even when fighting each other as the British and the Americans did in the Seven

Years' War, the American Revolution and in 1812. Walter Russell Mead says he freely acknowledges that in one respect those he calls "Waspophobes" are right:

> The Anglo-Americans do in fact have a secret master plan to dominate the world, and they have been following it faithfully for three hundred years. During that time Britain and the United States have been willing and able to adhere to a unique approach to world politics that has consistently led the English-speaking powers to greater success in world affairs than their rivals.

The secret plan, Mead says, is "embedded in the assumptions, habits, and institutions of the English-speaking powers". This Anglo-Saxon moral culture is what drove the British Empire and what drove the Americans to take over from that empire in terms of economic and military power in the last century. It is worth adding that Americans who stress their ties with Britain tend in the modern world to be those who harbour the greatest suspicion about their fellow US citizens. They accept that for some time the majority of Americans have not been descended from English-speaking ancestors. Nevertheless, these Anglos point out what they claim is an eternal truth: America, *the idea,* is an English one and all the successive genera-tions of immigrants who have washed up on America's shores have, perhaps unconsciously, signed up for that. They have been bequeathed the great gift of honorary metaphorical English ancestry.

This belief is fascinating because it suggests that for as long as America is America there will be a corner of it, even a *cornerstone* of it, that is forever England. Unless they go mad and multicultural, they will stay English even when no one has the foggiest idea where England is. As Arthur Schlesinger – once of President Kennedy's inner circle – put it when opposing multiculturalism in New York schools in the 1990s: "the British legacy has been modified, enriched, and reconstituted by the absorption of non-Anglo cultures and traditions as well as by the distinctive experiences of American life." And yet, he added, America's core is derived from Britain: "to pretend otherwise is to falsify history. To teach otherwise is to mislead our students."

So they need us after all? The special relationship, seen through this prism, is all that stands between America and, say, Brazil. Shorn of the Anglo pillar, America is just another large multicultural nation. It is a nation as well, not an idea. When America is an idea it has to be our idea, the idea of the English-speaking peoples. This does not, the thinking goes, mean that Americans have to be anglophiles in their individual tastes. They can think what they like about Olde England provided that they think in the manner dictated by the ties of kinship: respecting the rule of law, believing in representative government, in the ability of the individual to make a difference in the world, in the value of work. Of course, plenty of immigrants to America might think those things anyway, but assimilation into Britishness is still regarded by a large number of older-generation Americans as a sine qua non of the continuance of the dream. They do not call it the special relationship but that is what it is for them. Perhaps they should be more open about acknowledging it.

There is, this analysis suggests, no fundamental difference between the core values, the psychological wellsprings of the American mind and the British. We are all dependent on the attributes I have just listed but also, in a more general sense, on the open society in which tradition is challenged, and above all, on a philosophical tradition that regards history as progress – open-ended and never closing down, part and parcel of being human. Walter Russell Mead cites the problem of the cows, as posed by G. K. Chesterton. Cows have a long history in the sense that they have been around a long time. Much has happened to them. But not much of this has been driven by them, and although they comprise different breeds with differing ways of life, they have never consciously struggled against each other or, indeed, come together to improve their lot. As Chesterton said, "a history of cows in twelve volumes would not be very lively reading". Our history is lively because of what humans, uniquely, bring to it, and Mead suggests that the Anglo-Americans understand this best. They are not trapped in the vision of history that has us all ending up like cows, all issues resolved. Anglo-Americans understand (in spite of some evidence to the contrary) that there is more to life than ending history in a neat all-ends-tied-up and all-conflicts-resolved pasture.

Surely he is right, at least about the Americans. The misapprehension that America is about easy living and nothing else has been nailed a thousand times. Greatness – riches and all that come with them – is not achieved through the pursuit of comfort and wealth, the search for nicer pastures and nothing more than that. American energy has much deeper and more interesting roots. It is, as Mead puts it, "a quest for meaning".

But are both nations really still strivers after meaning to the same extent? In truth, it seems to me that the nation I left still is, while the nation I have come home to is not. Although it is quite true that both have a tendency in their histories and their national myths to cleave to a view of history as progress and themselves as drivers of progress, the Americans do not appear to have lost that sense, whereas we British are increasingly happy to be the cows in the field. The defence review conducted soon after the coalition government came to power felt like evidence of this. Much to the upset of the military men, and in particular the naval men, the review was really about saving money. It had little of vision about it. We were told that Britain was going to continue to harass baddies around the world but that, ahem, there would be a pause while we sorted out whether we could get any jets to fly off our aircraft carriers. And those carriers were being built (it was pretty obvious to all) only because to cancel them would be too costly. I never got the sense, chairing discussions on the subject on the *Today* programme, that anyone outside the military really cared much about the wider strategic questions the review really should have been raising. Were we leaders, still, or led? Do we have a unique contribution to make to the world or not? Since we still have money if we choose to find it, why did we not choose to find it?

Of course, it goes far wider than mere military ambition, this quiescence in the face of history. It seeps into the soul. It is an attitude that allows the other fellow's point of view to move up the scale from being interesting and informative to being admirable and enviable and right. British conversation about the outside world has become apologetic. I do not suggest that the payouts to the former Guantanamo detainees were an overt case of surrender – this was a legal decision taken after credible evidence of maltreatment was provided – but I did get the sense that the general shrugging of shoulders afterwards was part and parcel of an attitude that feels comfortable with the idea that we *should* be apologising.

I make no claim that Britain has entirely given up the ghost. There is certainly a widely held view in Britain that aspects of our national life are decent and worthy of worldwide respect. London is a far more open-minded city than Washington or New York and Londoners are rightly proud of it. But in the longer term, we do not self-consciously see ourselves as leaders. In terms of zest for the fight – the fight for history, the fight to make the world bend to your way of thinking – a suggestion that the English-speaking peoples still shoulder this burden together is a little wide of the mark. The Americans have left us behind; it is one of the reasons why we find them so annoying, so sure of themselves, so outrageously (embarrassingly) old-fashioned and imperial in outlook. They look like we once did, but no longer do.

They need gently to be reined in; they need to reconnect with a realisation previous American generations had: that military might is useless without internal strength. Libya and the reluctance of the Americans to lead the way in ousting Colonel Gaddafi might be part of the beginning of this process. So I am not suggesting a kind of Venus and Mars split in the future, with the plucky Americans fighting and the rest of us enjoying the fruits of victory. I do think America, when this mid-life crisis passes, will have to fight less and think more imaginatively about how power can be used around the world. But for now it is simply worth noting that the history of the United States thus far has led them down a path in which a self-assured willingness to put enemies to the sword is part of their DNA and needs to be channelled rather than denied or denigrated. America is still armed to the teeth and still believes strongly in its right to defend itself and attack its enemies where possible. And it is worth adding that many Americans think they inherited this DNA *from us!*

How special is that?

Chapter Eight

Britain is a proud, independent nation with a
distinct sense of our own values and traditions,
many of which are very sharply different and, in
some cases, contradictory to America's.
Peter Oborne, *Daily Telegraph*, May 2011

Forget Europe wholly, your veins throb with blood,
to which the dull current in her is but mud.
Let her sneer, let her say your experiment fails,
in her voice there's a tremble, e'en now while
she rails..
Robert Lowell, "A Fable for Critics"

Chapter LXII: A Bad Thing
America was thus clearly top nation, and History
came to a
W.C. Sellar and R.J. Yeatman, *1066 and All That*

HERE IS AN IRONY: although the big set-piece events in American politics are far more distant from the grass-roots than ours, although the speeches are formulaic and often an amalgam of stuff that has already been tested to destruction in previous appearances, there is one important respect in which their politics is far more grounded than ours. This is where I wonder whether the Thatcher speech quoted in the last chapter – in a way uncontroversial and boilerplate – was actually a fundamental misreading of them and us, a misreading that the modern age is showing up as never before.

British statesmen and women, reaching for their thesauruses to find new terms for the closeness of our systems and the commonality of our heritage, commit a fallacy. They misunderstand American democracy. American democracy is people based. It is not, at its heart, representative. What I mean by this is that Americans have never really trusted their representatives to exercise their own independent judgement. American representatives are meant to channel the views of the people. Their own views don't matter much.

Here is the British view, pretty much unchanged since Edmund Burke's speech to the electors of Bristol in 1774, in which he told them in no uncertain terms that he reserved the right, in Parliament, to use his own judgement and to do so without apology. It is a famous passage and worth quoting in full:

> To deliver an opinion, is the right of all men; that of constituents is a weighty and respectable opinion, which a representative ought always to rejoice to hear; and which he ought always most seriously to consider. But *authoritative* instructions; *mandates* issued, which the member is bound blindly and implicitly to obey, to vote, and to argue for, though contrary to the clearest conviction of his judgment and conscience, these are things utterly unknown to the laws of this land, and which arise from a fundamental mistake of the whole order and tenor of our constitution.

This has never been the American way. It is a simple matter of fact that the American political tradition stems at least in part from British history – Magna Carta and the idea of limits on the authority of the ruler, and of representative government in a general sense. The history books are full of these parallels and direct lines of descent, tracing the institutional ancestry of the American way back to the English, to the Puritans and the Glorious Revolution. But look at us now! Are we really that similar? When we talk about democracy, are we really talking about the same thing? Robert Southey, a traveller to America in 1809, wrote that the Americans have "a distinct national character, and even a national physiognomy." American heads were a different shape. He was right, I think.

The fact is that Americans believed long before most Britons did in democracy meaning the rule of all. To justify slavery, they convinced themselves that slaves were fundamentally different. But all those inside the tent were to be treated as equals. There was no other way. Majority rule was invented there, not here in the UK, and it shows. But they also believed from the outset in majority rule – or anyone's rule – being strictly limited. Their tradition is anti-government in a way that really owes more to the taming of the prairies than to the small print of Magna Carta. One of the oddities of American history is why the welfare state – the habits and the theory of support for the poorest – never took off in the US. The reason for this is that alongside a belief in democracy, Americans maintained from the beginning a belief in self-help and individual betterment. As one nineteenth-century American magazine put it:

> Legislation has been the fruitful parent of nine-tenths of all the evils, moral and physical, by which mankind has been afflicted since the creation of the world, and by which human nature has been self degraded, fettered, and oppressed.

We British have never thought that. Not when kings ruled, not when parliamentary democracy was taking off, and not now when we are all in it together. We legislate to improve. Our tradition is utterly different. Look at the grief Lady Thatcher still gets for suggesting that society does not exist separately from families. Americans dislike government but when it has to exist they keep it close to them in their states or neighbourhoods. We rather like government; we enjoy being governed. We are way, way too busy to get involved. "Politicians are all the same," we say, meaning: let them get on with it because we have a bus to catch. We are so lazy! We have never really governed ourselves or shown any interest in it. We are happy for administrative classes to develop and flourish and decay and smell nasty and then be replaced by others – quangos or people's peers. We have no pressure for term limits (a feature of American political debate) or sense of ownership of our tribunes. The rhetoric, post-expenses scandal, is about seizing the process, revivifying politics, getting involved. The reality, to my eyes, is that we don't really want to.

So our political closeness to the Americans is to some extent a sham. The British wit and writer of the 1930s, Phillip Guedalla, used to say that any American ambassador to London had to use the meaningless term "glorious heritage" when describing any aspect of

UK–US affairs – and stick very much to that heritage and history rather than modern issues or modern-day American achievements in any field: "in general it is undesirable that he should confess awareness of any author subsequent to the Declaration of The Independence!"

The ambassador could be rude – tread on toes, a sign of him being in the family – so that, in the words of Guedalla, "he ministers to the complete misunderstanding that is the sole safeguard against war between the US and UK".

The historian William Clark, writing in 1957, said: "The most significant fact about the development of Britain's attitude to America is that it began in humiliation which was later tempered by oblivion."

Oblivion! Those who prate about our closeness forget the historical evidence that for much of the time the United States has been alive we Brits have ignored it.

The Americans used to complain. Senator Lodge wrote to A. J. Balfour in 1896: "You have kept yourselves in a state of ignorance about the United States. Until very recently your newspapers gave it less space than to Belgium or Holland. Surely this was not wise." This American upset at a lack of proper recognition persisted for much longer than you might think. In 1953, the *New York Tribune's* London correspondent wrote that press coverage in the United Kingdom was "altogether inadequate to enable British readers to follow the major events of the United States and express any intelligent opinions about them".

Could we, in fact, have been enemies? Might the English-speaking peoples have been fractured in a way that would make talk of mutual bonds of history look utterly hollow and false? We certainly fell out during the revolution and in the war of 1812, during which the British burned the White House to the ground. Throughout that period there was a nationalistic fervour in America that was decidedly anti-British, with a sense that the British were merely waiting for an opportunity to damage and destroy the upstart nation. And the upstart nation fought back – in particular with school textbooks that taught that Britain was a force for malignancy, not the wellsspring of common values. William Clark writes of a visit to a Midwestern school in 1938, where he overheard a speech by a ten-year-old: "Britain owes us her national existence, which we saved in the last war; she owes us her empire which we fought to preserve; she owes us billions of dollars in war debts – and what do we get? Gratitude? No – insults!"

Throughout the nineteenth century, it is fair to say that Britain and America were really in the business of falling out more than celebrating the commons bonds of heritage. The process was aided by the influx of anti-British Irish immigrants in the 1840s, but more than anything else, it was caused by the mishandling of the American Civil War, during which Britain managed to fall out with both sides. It was said at the time that a war with Britain was the only thing that could have united the armies of Grant for the North, and Lee for the South.

America was angry then for much of the nineteenth century and Britain was the focus. As Rudyard Kipling, who lived in America, put it: "England was still the dark and dreadful enemy to be feared and guarded against." And towards the end of the century, as America was getting powerful as well as angry, it was with Britain that it nearly went to war. The cause of this potentially history-altering spat was Venezuela.

The problem was a border dispute between British Guyana and Venezuela, a dispute given added zest by the presence of gold in the disputed area. The British still had the power to seize land anywhere in the world and the threat was clear: that they would put Venezuela in its place and by extension point out to the Americans the limits of their power and influence.

The Americans cited the Monroe Doctrine under which, according to them, no European power had the right to lord it over South America. This was the United States' backyard. The response from the British was imperious – Lord Salisbury, the Prime Minister, wrote a lecturing letter to the Americans, in which he airily pointed out that the Doctrine had not been accepted by Britain or indeed anyone else. High-handedness from a lord! So British. And guaranteed down the ages to get the Americans upset.

A wave of patriotic fervour swept the United States and Congress was asked by the President to send its own commission to Venezuela with the power to adjudicate on the disputed land and enforce the outcome. The *New York Sun* carried the headline "War if Necessary!" and some even talked about taking Canada while they were about it. For a week it looked like war. Fratricidal or civil war, some said, but war nonetheless. In the end it did not happen, thanks at least in part to a sense in both nations that it would have been an odd and rather unseemly conflict – an absurdity as well as a crime, as Joseph Chamberlain called it – but still the fact remains that war was on the cards. No bond of friendship prevented the two nations from coming to the brink: indeed the opposite; the hostility that had simmered since the beginning could still be brought to the boi at any moment.

It was imperialism, not a love of democracy, that brought the United States and Britain together. The Americans, shortly after the Venezuela business was resolved, got the taste for foreign conflict and foreign dominion. It began over the Spanish possession of Cuba and the Philippines. After a nasty incident in Cuba, in which an American warship was blown up, the Americans and the Spanish went to war. The end result was Cuba's independence and – for the first time since the Declaration of Independence – American invasion and domination of a foreign nation; the Philippines. The history of America's Philippine venture could hardly be less glorious; it resulted in appalling suppression of local nationalists, in which many thousands of civilians were killed. It was an utter mess – one of those lessons of history that only historians seem to notice.

But at the time others noticed and drew rather fabulous conclusions about the significance of the Philippines to Anglo-American friendship. Finally the Yanks were showing themselves to be real men, or to be more precise, real White Men.

Kipling, impressed as never before, wrote his famous poem "The White Man's Burden" as a direct response to the Spanish–American war. "Take up the White Man's Burden" was an exhortation aimed directly at the Americans. Kipling was not alone. A motley collection of Englishmen and Americans hoped that this was the moment to seize the initiative and – incredibly, given the history of the nineteenth century – to link our nations together once again.

Lord Cromer, for instance, excited by the temporary annexation of Cuba by the United States, declared his support because "I want the world to see that Anglo-Saxons can govern a decadent Latin race". Cromer was a former Consul General in Egypt and a believer in the White Man's Burden (and it was definitely "Man's" – he ended his days heading the National League for Opposing Woman Suffrage) but he was by no means a lone eccentric. Proposals were made for a union of greater Britain – Cecil Rhodes among those in the vanguard. There was to be an imperial federation of all English-speaking peoples. By the end of the century, the idea was attracting notable, if not widespread, support. In 1898, Joseph Chamberlain called for the Stars and Stripes and the Union Jack to wave together over an Anglo-Saxon alliance. The establishment of a colonial office in Washington was predicted. The imperial enthusiast Rhodes was agitating behind the scenes for what he called "the ultimate recovery of the United States as an integral part of the British Empire". To this end he proposed that there should be an imperial parliament that might sit for some time in London and for some in Washington.

As ever, Kipling found the words: "After a nation has pursued certain paths alone in the face of some slight misrepresentation, it is consoling to find another nation (which one can address without a dictionary) preparing to walk along the same lines to, I doubt not, the same ends."

The nation that once lowered the magazine postal rate to Canada to try to stop American cultural domination (take that, Hollywood) was now at least partly in love with the idea of a permanent union. Of course, in the end it came to nothing, and in the coming to nothing there was and is a message for those who preach that we and they are one. The lesson is: we are not one. Never were, since the inception. The truth is that the colonists had grown apart from the old country long before they declared their independence, and nothing could ever or can ever bring us together. The American backers of the reunification of the English-speaking peoples, few in number, represented a strand in American politics rather than any kind of national feeling. The most prominent of these was probably the newspaper editor W. T. Stead. Stead wanted to "realize the great idea of race union" by merging the British Empire and the United States under essentially US control. Stead was no loony. He wrote convincingly and presciently about the domination of American culture and was one of the first to point out that its power lay (as it lies still) in its ability to seduce rather than in any forced adaptation. But Stead was not backed by supporters of a similar calibre. Rather, they were the *Mayflower* folk; upset at the swarm of Irish and Italian and other hyphenated Americans landing on America's shores. They were worried about race and colour and as such were somewhat un-American. They were the Lord Cromers of the United States, though in a much tinier minority than even the noble Lord was in Britain.

It was never going to happen, this remarriage of the English-speaking peoples. Stead died on the Titanic, aptly enough. The First World War and the changes it brought to the balance of world power, and to thinking about imperialism and war and culture more generally, put paid to the remnants of the scheme, if a scheme it ever genuinely was. Randolph Bourne, now largely a forgotten figure but at the time of the First World War an important public intellectual, decided that "the good things in the American temperament and institutions were not English but were the fruit of our superior cosmopolitanism". Bourne wanted America to become – in the modern parlance – multicultural rather than a nation of settlers who sign on for the Anglo-Saxon world-view and self-view. He saw America teaching the

British and the rest of the world a lesson. This vision of the role of the United States – as teacher and leader and exemplar – ranged from the anti-war and anti-intervention Bourne through to writers and thinkers and politicians across the political spectrum. America came of age in the early part of the last century; the British and the Americans spent the century before as enemies, came together in the heads of the imperialists for a tiny sliver of time at the dawn of the new age (the White House flew flags at half-mast on the death of Queen Victoria – a first), but then diverged suddenly and decisively at around the time of the First World War. Political union was not to be.

And soon the ignorance and dismissiveness at the hands of the Brits that the Americans used to complain of was very much a reverse phenomenon. F. Scott Fitzgerald wrote after the war that the entire continent of Europe was now "of merely antiquarian interest". We had ignored them in the past and now they were returning the favour. This was the beginning of American insouciance about the details of the rest of the world, an insouciance that, to the disappointment of some of his keener European fans, did not die with the arrival of President Obama. Far from it. I remember horror among the Brits on the Obama press plane on his first trip to the UK, shortly after becoming President. We opened our White House briefings on the nation we were visiting and discovered that the opening gambit, the central fact about the dear old mother country, was that it was "slightly smaller than Oregon"! And we didn't really learn much more – some stuff about the Romans and modern-day friendship, but that was that. Oregon has a population of under four million and a contribution to the history of the world that is, it is fair to say, not yet worthy of much study. Lord Cromer would be revolving in his grave at the enormity of the snub. Now, to be fair to the White House, size does matter to Americans, because they have a hazy idea of the relative bulk of European states and after a night on a plane and arriving at Stansted you need to be broken in gently. But even so, the land of Shakespeare and Milton and Wellington and Churchill reduced to this: *slightly smaller than Oregon*. Years before, I had been with President Bush on a visit to Belfast. The press pack then had referred to the destination as "Ireland". We were indeed on the island of Ireland, but did they not grasp that there was an important distinction – in fact that that distinction was what all the fuss was about? From Bush to Obama and beyond; they do not really take our disputes seriously any more than they have respect for the size of our land mass. We are small and old and frail.

There are some Americans who cling to the Britishness of their culture, largely because they feel out of sorts with the people who have just moved into their neighbourhood. True political Americanism, as it were, is something alien to Britain. It is not – absolutely not – a kind of free-market, anything-goes attitude to life that some on the left equate with American values. It is more complex and nuanced than that – focused on limited government and extraordinary social energy, sometimes linked to government and sometimes not. But this energy and this zest for practical betterment and openness to talent is not British.

It hurts. The English-speaking peoples indeed. Robert Lowell's "blood and mud" jibe echoes down the years. History is on his side. Our political cultures are much less connected than we sometimes think and are becoming less connected by the day. At the end of the Obama visit to London in 2011, the political commentator Peter Oborne was almost alone, but entirely right, in my view, in suggesting that the treatment of the President had verged on the sycophantic: sinister, he called it. Oborne pointed out that when the relationship between our nations really was special – or essential – there had been no need for all the flummery of a state visit. No post-war president had been granted one until George W. Bush. None had needed one perhaps, nor this pretence that we and they are hewn from the same political and social rock. There is a foolishness – a brittle quality – to our modern-day efforts to claim we are all on the same page, all the time. We are not. And we never have been.

Chapter Nine

Facts are stubborn things; and whatever may be
our wishes, our inclinations, or the dictates of our passion,
they cannot alter the state of facts and evidence.
John Adams, "Argument in Defense of the Soldiers
in the Boston Massacre Trials", December 1770

Felix, qui potuit rerum cognoscere causas.
(Fortunate is he who is able to know the meaning of things)
Virgil, *Georgics*, 29BC

WHEN I ARRIVED at the London School of Economics
in the early 80s I was interested in opinions. By the
time I left I was interested in facts. The LSE motto is
the second half of that quotation from the Latin poet
Virgil: "to know the meaning (or the causes) of things."
Of course, I learned what we all eventually grasp: that in
the social sciences and indeed in science, generally the

latter, the meanings or causes, cannot be finally separated from the former, the subjective opinions of men and women, but the idea of evidence-based civilisation appealed to me and it still does. It is not a holy grail; the LSE's greatest teacher, Michael Oakeshott, said it better than anyone else: "In political activity men sail a boundless and bottomless sea; there is neither harbour for shelter nor floor for anchorage, neither starting point nor appointed destination." But part of the key to successful bobbing about, if that is what we are in the business of doing, is the use of rational appreciation of generally accepted facts. What I did not realise during my student days is how delicate the flower of rational decision-making really is, even in (*especially* in?) the supposedly modern, post-ideological developed world. The mindset that took the LSE to Libya in the early part of this century shows how easy it is, even in a centre of academic learning, to see rationality suspended. In the UK and in America, we have grappled in modern times with policy formulation based on ideology and based on rationality. On both sides of the Atlantic, most serious policy is purported to be an effort to engage with the facts as reasonable people might see them. The issue of bankers' bonuses is a good example: policy-makers might disagree at heart over whether or not bankers deserve a kicking, but the argument tends to be practical: what effect will a new regime have on the ability of the banks to benefit the taxpayer in the longer term? So the argument still rages – kick them or not kick them – but with a framework of facts to be used on either side. The nature of the facts can, of course, be debated, but the relevance of facts, the importance of the argument over who is right and who is wrong, still looms large. In much of the world, imagined conspiracies, religious convictions and state-imposed ideology play a much greater role. The small point then is that Britain and America are similar in this respect and on both sides of the Atlantic we should be grateful.

But the bigger point is this: for how much longer? In eight years' reporting from America I saw what increasingly looks like a new revolution taking the nation in a direction far removed from the intellectual traditions of the LSE or indeed John Adams. As with all revolutions, the one I am thinking about began long before it was noticed. You sensed it, if at all, as one senses an unexplained breeze that ruffles the hair or causes a newspaper to take flight and flutter into the distance, before stillness returns, fooling you into a false sense of calm. What was that? you wonder. Is there a storm brewing? And then you go about your business and forget.

One such moment: I was in the office of a former congressman and I was interviewing him on the subject of the Bush administration and science. The President was still in his first term, Iraq was still un-invaded, but those who believed in actions being taken only after "the meaning of things" was properly known were feeling nervous. I had gone to see this man to get him to defend a White House decision to pack a committee offering scientific advice on the efficacy of a morning-after pill known as Plan B with people who had no scientific standing. I will not bore you with the details of the arguments but the point of the story is this: the former congressman was amiable and courteous and absolutely unshakable in this view: that folks in Harvard and Yale were, in the future, going to have to share their influence on science policy and the assessment of scientific evidence with folks off the street in Boise, Idaho.

It seemed a quaint idea. America was certainly not in every sense an evidence-based society, but President Bush's men surely had some respect for facts, for that tradition of evidence-based policy-making I referred to at the start of this chapter?

I have to say that the conclusion of our radio documentary was that their respect was limited: often rhetorical rather than real. And in the post-documentary

and post-Bush world it seems to me that the relationship between American politics and journalism and
American learning and scholarship – between opinion
and fact – has become ever more tenuous.

How can this still hold true after the arrival of
President Obama, who is in many respects the most
academic of modern presidents, indeed one often
described as professorial to a fault? However disa-
pointing he has been to many Americans, this
president is science-interested and science-aware. When
I interviewed him for the BBC in 2009, we were talking
before the cameras went on and I mentioned to him
that I had a son who had recently been diagnosed with
Type One Diabetes, a rare and unpleasant autoimmune
condition. President Bush (a man I always found very
decent and engaging one to one) would have teared up
or grasped my shoulders and offered a prayer. President
Obama offered advice – and a percentage chance that
it could be cured in ten years. To be honest, at that
moment he knew more about it than I did.

So the President is a believer in knowing the
meaning of things. But the President is one man and,
as I think we all know now, he does not find it easy
to take his nation where he wants it to go. America,
in the years I worked there, fell out of love with facts
and research, in particular with inconvenient facts and

discomforting research. The coming of Obama did not change that.

The late Senator Daniel Moynihan once issued a warning to Americans that they were entitled to their own opinions but not their own facts. At the time he spoke, it seemed a reasonable point of view. Now it looks deeply anachronistic. Along with the battering of the scientific establishment, we have seen in America a broadcasting environment where left and right fight nightly battles from their respective castles (Fox for the right and MSNBC for the left) and where the middle ground (CNN and the old broadcast news programmes) are caught in the crossfire, arrows raining down on their unprotected heads. They are slaughtered in the ratings and (crucially) in public affection, seen as folks who cannot get off the fence, cannot admit their own biases. The cable channels were never subject to the Fairness Doctrine – introduced in 1949, in which the broadcast channels were forced to be impartial or to pretend to be – but the demise of the doctrine in 1987 certainly assisted in creating a general atmosphere in which balance is seen as a weasel word, associated with stodgy, dishonest mediocrity, while jagged, nakedly partisan reportage is seen as laudable and clean. Fox's slogan – *we report, you decide* – is gorgeously Orwellian. Nobody among the audiences of America's most successful cable news shows, either on the left or on the right, is doing any deciding, in the sense of making choices based on a fair-minded review of the evidence. But would-be providers of impartial news find themselves in a psychological bind. In a desperate effort to fight off those who regard them as just as biased as everyone else but merely less honest, they become trapped in the timidity and faux impartiality of the "on the one hand, on the other hand" school of reportage that sees any drivel spouted by anyone as equally valid. They have lost the safe space they once had. The suggestion that they simply compete in the market place (as, say, *The Economist* does very happily in the world of news magazines) misses the point that broadcasting reaches and shapes a national debate in a way no print media does.

This general attitude towards truth pervades much of American public life. People talk past each other. If someone comes up with some evidence, someone else trashes it. Nobody believes anybody or feels the remotest bit tempted to change their minds *when the facts change*, because they don't ever change their minds! America blogs rather than reads.

Not that this is quite as recent a development as I initially thought. American broadcasting is like the Wild West today but its past has been equally rough.

America, generally speaking, is a nation of folks too polite and gentle to say boo to a goose. A nation that says "My Gosh" rather than "My God". A nation where journalists stand when the President enters the room. A nation of white picket fences and neat flags and "Have a nice day" smiles.

So why do they appear to hate each other so much on TV?

Shortly before Barack Obama was elected, I was in Ohio interviewing people outside a Republican rally. A woman with two young children said she would be happy to talk.

"Why do you dislike Obama?" I asked.

"Because he is a baby killer!"

The woman's hatred of abortion had morphed into a hatred of those who believed in abortion rights. It was bizarre; chilling. But it was a sign of what was to come.

The right-wing Tea Party movement is a symptom of this crisis but I do not believe it is necessarily the cause. It is true that some Tea Party folk hate Barack Obama but the movement is a consequence of something much deeper and more worrying for all Americans: they kinda hate themselves.

A nation where self-belief comes with the apple pie has fallen into a slough of despond. The Tea Party members are not bad people, most of them, but they are deeply worried people. And when people are worried – frightened even – they tend to hit out. That is why the language of politics has become so dreadful in America: Americans are full of dread. They hate themselves for their inability to get out of the mess they are in.

Americans are seriously concerned that their nation is in a horrible decline; living standards, power abroad, everything heading for collapse. Because Obama is in office he takes a lot of the flak and a lot of unfair flak – no question about that.

But when Bush was in power I had a friend who was a relative of his. He (and the family) were devastated by the personal attacks on George W. In particular I remember a piece in a fancy news magazine by a prominent left-wing journo that began: "I hate President Bush!"… and spent hundreds of words backing that up with reasons that included, I seem to remember, "the way he walks!"

So it is not new, this hatred that scars American politics. In fact, you could argue it is a glorious American tradition: when the nation goes downhill the language of politics goes crazy. A good example from history is the broadcasting of Father Charles Coughlin. Few remember him today, but Coughlin was the conservative motormouth of the 1930s – he had a massive talk radio presence and was a severe irritant to President Roosevelt. Charles Coughlin was a self-populist nutcase not unlike some of today's radio and TV stars. He probably cared more about himself than he genuinely did about the causes he espoused, but that did not blunt his ire. At the height of his powers – in the period before the Second World War – Coughlin was getting 40 million regular listeners. You could walk down American streets and hear his voice coming from every home. And what he was telling his listeners was poisonous – he was a Nazi. At a rally after the war, he famously made his hatred of the Jews clear: "When we get through with the Jews in America, they'll think the treatment they received in Germany was nothing."

In the end, Roosevelt censored him. Coughlin was suppressed, pure and simple. His radio broadcasts were deemed unlicensed and he was banned from sending material through the post. It was not pretty and it was not freedom. And it led, after a few years, to the Fairness Doctrine, which forced all American broadcasters to give space to opposing arguments and to strive for impartiality – as we are still required to in Britain – over a reasonable period. In 1987 the doctrine was repealed and the rest is history. Interestingly, America does not have a new Charles Coughlin but the time is ripe. (Some say the Fox broadcaster Glenn Beck comes close although, in fact, he does not make overt threats to any identified group)

Britain feels mighty academic and calm in comparison. Tony Blair, Lady Thatcher and, I suppose, Gordon Brown get a battering, but in general one of the joys of coming back to the UK has been the richness of its political debate. This may sound odd to the jaded British public who associate their MPs with the abuse of expenses and their constitution with sclerosis and only stuttering tentative reform. But we are – it seems to me – still, on the whole, respecters of evidence and the cool debate that comes with that respect. When the LSE academic Tony Travers comes on the *Today* programme to talk about local government, the audience accept and appreciate his standing as an expert whose opinions are based on firm foundations. They accept that even if he is fallible, he does, to a greater extent than is the case with most of us on this subject, "know the meaning of things."

Do the UK's broadcasting impartiality rules help? My sense is that they might. If Tony Travers were competing with a Fox News-type alternative, the dynamic would change – some kind of spurious "balance" would have to be sought out. And nobody would believe him anyway, because respect for alternative views would have been lost.

We are a little way away from the end of Tony Travers. But our current broadcasting rules are going to come under great pressure in coming years, becoming increasingly difficult to defend in terms of freedom or practicability in the world of multimedia offerings and multi-device consumption. How can you justify government imposed rules that constrain the broadcaster's material that you are watching on your iPad but no rules at all on the YouTube content you are watching on the very same device? I confess it is a tricky argument to make.

But the evidence from America suggests that in my line of work in the modern digital world, the search for truth will be replaced by the dictates of "truthiness", which as fans of the American comedian Stephen Colbert will know, is something completely different. Truthiness was a mock-word introduced by Colbert when the Bush administration was in its pomp to describe a truth that was not based on facts but was felt in the gut. In a sense truthiness was a word that summed up a moment in American life – the moment when Afghanistan seemed to have been a successful venture and Iraq was not yet invaded – that unipolar moment when America seemed to be a newly woken giant able to cast its enemies to the four winds. But truthiness has outlived the hubris of those days. It stalks America still and its stalking is a warning to Britain: you can make a bonfire of the restrictions that enmeshed the news media in the age of Morecambe and Wise and you may well feel a rush of freedom-loving, devil-may-care *joie de vivre* when you do it. But there is a reckoning. When you openly acknowledge that opinions dominate the airwaves, you may create a space that is fundamentally altered. And when you suggest to people that there will still be those who pursue impartiality as a goal, you may well find a response that is troubling and unexpected. As a former chairman of the BBC, Michael Grade, put it:

> It could be that, in the context of this new world of opinionated, value-laden broadcasting, the BBC would be perceived not as fundamentally different from other providers, but as fundamentally the same. Not a proud beacon of impartiality and accuracy, but just another vehicle for another set of opinions and another value-system.

Occasionally in America, politicians notice this poisoning of the media well and try (always in vain) to have their fairness rules reimposed. Some big names including the former presidential candidate

John Kerry, have been interested in the idea. But it will never happen. The move, once made, can never be unmade. In the UK we have a choice to make and the results of that choice will determine far more certainly how American we are (and how American we become) than if we occasionally say "sidewalk" instead of "pavement"or "good" instead of "fine".

We could accept the arguments of those who claim that freedom demands that the airwaves hum to the sound of opinion. In particular, we could be persuaded by the notion that a distinction between what you watch on the TV at ten with Huw and what you browse (at the same time) on YouTube can sensibly be made in the longer term. I have no idea what the outcome of this debate should be or will be. It is not for me as a BBC reporter to render an opinion. But I do suggest that the moment we embrace American practice in this area, we embrace all that comes with it, Charles Coughlin, Glenn Beck and all. So to fuss about Americanisation but at the same time allow an end to our impartiality rules is to fail to see the wood for the trees. So here is another of those areas where they could have learned from us, and we can still learn from their mistakes – if mistakes they are – before it's too late.

Chapter Ten

> Why, after trampling upon the honour of our country, and
> representing it as little better than a land of barbarism —
> why, we say, perpetually trample also upon the very grammar
> of our language, and make that appear as Gothic as, from
> your description, our manners are rude? — Freely, good sir,
> will we forgive all your attacks, impotent as they are illiberal,
> upon our national character; but for the future spare — O
> spare, we beseech you, our mother-tongue!
> **Message from the English to the Americans in**
> ***The European Magazine, and London Review*, 1797**

IN MY FIRST WEEK back in Britain presenting the *Today* programme, I glanced at the clock and announced to a bemused nation that it was "a quarter of eight".

Guys, relax. Suck it up. Enjoy. Or not... I can reveal exclusively that many people did not enjoy the moment or feel able to suck it up. They were unrelaxed for several days afterwards.

American English – Americanisms generally – reduce otherwise reasonable, rational folks to neuralgia and worse. "What's the weather going forward?" – to me a perfectly comprehensible question – would cause hernias in the *Today* office. Dudes, I remind them: "Y'all need to know that I spent eight years in the US, my children grew up there, and a subtle change in the language has kinda seeped in."

Part of me understands exactly why it can be so annoying to us Brits. We invented the confounded language, after all. We perfected it; our ancestors fought the wars and established the culture that made it such a worldwide force, so why should we see it barbecued and handed back with tomato sauce on top? What was wrong with it raw? The (normally) gentle and deeply cultured journalist Matthew Engel put it like this in a piece in the *Mail on Sunday*:

> Old buffers like me have always complained about the process, and we have always been defeated. In 1832, the poet Samuel Taylor Coleridge was fulminating about the "vile and barbarous" new adjective that had just arrived in London. The word was "talented". It sounds innocuous enough to our ears, as do "reliable", "influential" and "lengthy", which all inspired loathing when they first crossed the Atlantic. But the process gathered speed with the arrival of cinema and television

in the 20th Century. And in the 21st it seems unstoppable. The US-dominated computer industry, with its "licenses", "colors" and "favorites" is one culprit. That ties in with mobile phones that keep 'dialing' numbers that are always "busy".

My dictionary (a mere 12 years old) defines "geek" as an American circus freak or, in Australia, "a good long look". We needed a word to describe someone obsessively interested in computer technology. It seems a shame there was never any chance of coining one ourselves. Nowadays, people have no idea where American ends and English begins. And that's a disaster for our national self-esteem. We are in danger of subordinating our language to someone else's – and with it large aspects of British life.

But having lived for so long in America and having heard my children speak American and watched them make the transition back to English, I want to make the case that there is much to be loved about the idioms of the New World. It is not all about laziness. It enriches as well as simplifies our mother tongue.

We tend to think of American English as a pointer to a lazier, quotidian future, in which a brainless homogeneity is achieved at the expense of rigour and linguistic crunch.

In American that might read: "We're all gonna talk the same."

But sometimes American English can surprise with its quaint, even dainty, formulations. When was the last time you were asked if you wanted a beverage? A *what*? It's a perfectly good word and we all know what it means but in English English it would be an odd way of buying someone a drink. In America, beverages are served on every street corner. Dr Pepper anyone?

I grew to love too the term "person of colour" meaning black or dark-skinned individual. Barack Obama has used it to great effect when talking about the newly prominent Republican Party leader, John Boehner. We are both, the President says, *people of colour*. The joke is that Mr Boehner is a white man who lives in Ohio (where the sun don't shine) but has a skin tone that suggests the frequenting of tanning salons or fancy foreign holiday destinations – and neither is good for Republican credibility.

I must admit that some American English is too chintzy even for my New World tastes. I hate the inability of Americans, in polite society, to call a spade a spade. A letter complaining about my defence of American English on a radio programme years ago pointed out, quite reasonably, that the results of this daintiness can sometimes be utterly ludicrous. The example the letter-writer gave was a natural history

programme she had seen in the US, in which a hippo-
potamus was said to be "going to the bathroom".

But still, when I hear my children speak American
English, I cannot help but smile. Stern-faced people
used to ask me and my wife about the efforts we were
making to help our kids lose their accents. None, we
would reply. They did it themselves and, to a large
extent, along with the accents have gone the idioms.

But just occasionally one will appear, like a shot of
Jack Daniels on a cold day. So although they speak
like the Queen, they can still be heard announcing that
they are "done" rather than "finished" or that their day
at school was "regular". They still struggle a bit with
English place names – Folkes*town* is my favourite –
but generally they are good. Sorry, fine.

The obvious advantage of American English is that
it is, to a much greater extent than English English,
genuinely classless. There used to be a suggestion that
Americans on the East Coast tended – mentally and
linguistically – to bow the knee to the old nations of
Europe; only Midwesterners were properly American.
It is certainly true that fashionable New York accents
from the 1950s sound oddly English. This is partly
because they fancied themselves as the Eurotrash of
the time and partly because they were simply a group
of people who had lived in one geographic region for

many years – other Americans were too new to their neighbourhoods to have any settled habits apart from godliness and a way with a Colt 45.

Those days are gone now and there is a wealth of American accents and language on the East Coast to put alongside the flat Midwestern, and of course the classic Southern drawl. Accents to Americans certainly suggest stuff. But never quite class stuff, in the British sense. Take the southerner. He or she drawls. "Why?" becomes "Whaaaa?"; "nail" becomes "nay-eel". Instead of saying "going to" he says "fixin' to". And the language slows. And life slows. Is this lower class? No way. A Southerner might be suspected of being a hang-over from *Gone with the Wind*, but his or her accent could put him or her up there in a starring role with the Rhetts and Scarletts, or down there with the slaves. You could not tell the difference from accent or from lexicon. And that is the same across the nation. Of course, educated Americans have more words at their disposal than do the uneducated. But the words used by all manner of folk will be far more similar than they are in Britain. And the head of state – be it George Bush or Barack Obama – will talk like the population. The Queen does not. After the announcement that Prince William's wedding day was to be a bank holiday, the papers were full of "day orf" headlines; how odd that the nation feels itself so utterly removed from the boss class that even the simplest word is pronounced differently. Sure, the Bushes mangled the language, but the language they were mangling was the same language that everyone else spoke. Do not misunderestimate the importance of this – to them and to us.

Did the Americans have to steal our language? It seems quite obvious to us now that they did; after all, most of the early settlers were from England. What could possibly persuade them to choose anything other than their mother tongue? Surely they never considered anything else? Actually, there is some suggestion that they did. In his masterly book *The American Language* (itself an effort to set out the case for the phenomenon it sought to describe), the great commentator H. L. Mencken mentions the hilarious (and possibly apocryphal) story of plans hatched during the revolution to abandon English as the national language for America and substitute Hebrew. Mencken adds that Greek was also reportedly considered but rejected on the grounds that "it would be more convenient for us to keep the language as it is, and make the English speak Greek". Whatever: the passion for independence led to a loathing for English authority in all areas including, well, English. Noah Webster, of Webster's dictionary fame, said after the revolution that Americans should "seize the present moment, and establish a national language as well as a national government. As an independent nation our honor requires us to have a system of our own, in language as well as government".

And that language was already being put into use. When Ben Franklin was sent to France as America's first ambassador, shortly after the Declaration of Independence, he was instructed by Congress to employ "the language of the United States". Franklin worked hard on the project. But even these early zealots stopped short of real big change (as they might have put it) as proposed by "a Scotchman of the name of Thornton". This man, Mencken notes, "having settled in the new republic and embraced its *Kultur* with horrible fervor, proposed a new alphabet even more radical than Franklin's. This new alphabet included e's turned upside down and i's with their dots underneath. 'Di Amerike languids,' he argued, 'uil des bi az distint az de gevernment, fri from aul foliz or enfilosofikel fasen.'"

Enough already. It did not catch on. But "Americanism" did and the man who coined the term, John Witherspoon, did not mean it as a compliment. Witherspoon was a keen member of the Continental Congress and no friend of the English, but in matters of language he was anything but a revolutionary. Mencken quotes him thus:

I have heard in this country," he wrote in 1781, "in the senate, at the bar, and from the pulpit, and see daily in dissertations from the press, errors in grammar, improprieties and vulgarisms which hardly any person of the same class in point of rank and literature would have fallen into in Great Britain.

One of the great complaints by the English of the Americans concerned the clarity of the new language. Imagine: anyone could speak it. One magazine sniffed that in American English the speakers thought "one word as good as another provided its meaning be clear." Gettoutahere!

The inanity of the British attack is obvious from some of the words the early Disgusteds of Tunbridge Wells complained about. "Lengthy" was one. Do some English patriots still avoid it?

The other irony of this century's linguistic battle is that many of the words the Brits complained about (and still do) were actually English words that had been brought over on the *Mayflower* but then discarded by the flighty English. They were, in fact, more English than the English. They were proper. But the English had forgotten them. These orphan words had been adopted by the colonists and had prospered in the colonies – like little English refugees, they had taken flight in the New World and were thus resented back at home.

Other words flowed from them to us over the years. Backwoodsman is all-American. So is caucus. And squatter. Some Americanisms are born but never go anywhere – they wither on the vine even in their home country. Mencken gives "cars" for railway carriages. Just occasionally you still hear it but the universal usage of the mid-nineteenth century was gone by the late twentieth and never made it to England. Not that anything in language is dead for ever. Dude, Mencken suggests, was born in 1883 but was dead by 1895. In 2010, in an interview with President Obama, the great Jon Stewart caused a stir by calling the Commander in Chief "dude" – but the upset was caused by the familiarity; the word is everywhere. Will it ever come to Britain? I doubt it; there is something about its easy familiarity that we might find difficult to take on board. David Cameron might be Dave but he will never be dude.

Similarly, the word "lot" meaning a parcel of land is easy and useful (and my children still ask whether we are leaving the car in a lot) but is oddly lacking from English English. Lot probably comes from the fact that early land allocation in the US was conducted by drawing lots. In that respect it is all-American. Do we complain about "lumber"? Lumber used to mean discarded furniture (lumber room) but now, to most Brits, it means cut trees. Are we the less for this change? Another infestation that my family would like to claim credit for, if it ever comes off, is the use of "store" instead of "shop". In America, a shop is somewhere you leave your car (the machine-shop), and a store is where you shop. In England, that is not the case and I see no real chance that it will become the case, in spite of my efforts in south London. Matthew Engel himself admits: "Almost all the parts of a car have different names in America, yet there is no sign of hood replacing bonnet, or the trunk supplanting the boot." That's freedom, Matthew! We can name our own parts. And when we like them, we can keep them.

And then, there are subtleties: road haulage is a good one. U Haul is one of the great American brands; you use it when you want to escape and do that reinventing we mentioned in Chapter One. You gather up all your belongings and pack them in a van that attaches to the back of your car. On the side of it are emblazoned the words U Haul. In English English, the meaning is obvious – someone is hauling this stuff somewhere and that person is you. And yet the word haul to Americans means something more: it means to take something somewhere by a means of transport. Road haulage, to an American, is tautological. Now we rub along with this difference but it is there, unresolved, like so much else in our linguistic relationship.

Another favourite – and this one is mentioned by Mencken – is that in America you are "sick" but in England you are "ill". "Doctor, I am sick" (in spite of sickies and sick notes) is a statement you would not hear in Tunbridge Wells. But sick is the original Anglo-Saxon word. For some reason the Puritans decided it was too vulgar and changed to the old Norse "ill". The Americans had started with sick and decided (rough, tough folks that they were) to stick with it. Actually, Mencken thinks it was probably to do with their Bibles: the colonists had few other books and could see no obvious point in changing them to accommodate a different word.

"I guess" is my final choice. Here is Shakespeare:

> Not all together; better far, I *guess,*
> That we do make our entrance several ways.
> *Henry VI*

You can't argue with the Bard.

I suppose, in fact, you can, but the argument seems to me a giant waste of time and energy, and one ulti-mately doomed to failure. Matthew Engel is left splut-tering by the sheer size of the task he has set himself and readers of the *Mail on Sunday* in turning back the tide. He understands that this is no small challenge, and towards the end of one of his linguistic pieces, he offers the doleful view that "the most effective remedy would be the abolition of 24-hour news channels and breakfast TV, both American imports of no merit". Oh, Matthew, believe me, my man – it ain't gonna happen.

Chapter Eleven

MY 81-YEAR-OLD UNCLE put his finger on it. We were discussing the Obama administration's lack of interest in Britain and the British, when Uncle Oliver pointed out an inconvenient truth: "Remember we didn't give a bugger about *them* until Alistair Cooke!"

He is right, of course. Before Churchill no serving British prime minister had set foot in the former colony. As the journalist Alexander Chancellor put it: "It is difficult to overestimate the ignorance of American history and culture that existed among most educated British people when Alistair Cooke started broadcasting…" Cooke introduced the British to their forgotten cousins in the manner of a gentle host at a rather restrained party. He did not assail his listeners with facts and figures – the nuts and bolts of America's rise to post-war pre-eminence, and Britain's mirror image decline – but instead concentrated on what he called "the springs of American life, whose bubbles are the headlines".

Justin Webb

Those were the words he used in his letter to the
BBC suggesting *Letter from America* and once the series
was commissioned, that was exactly the approach he
adopted. This was not idle chat – far from it – but
nor was it breathless reportage or relentless polemic.
Alistair Cooke told stories. He created images. He let
the listeners do the rest. And as they listened, so they
learned and wondered and thought about America, not
as simply a bigger, duller, coarser version of Britain, but
as a land of staggering variety and cultural significance:
a land worthy of exploration. *Letter From America* –
there were 2,869 separate editions – went on to be the
longest-running commentary programme the world
has ever known and, in terms of British–US relations,
one of the most important cultural links. Alistair
Cooke was an Englishman who became, gradually
but inexorably, an American, and did so over such a
lengthy period that you hardly noticed it happening.
He did not set out to persuade British listeners that
the US was the world's top nation. He certainly did
not suggest that it was without problems. In the course
of *Letter From America* plenty of disasters befell his
adopted land and none was brushed under the carpet.
But as well as an all-seeing eye, Alistair had a kindli-
ness about him which, when he bathed America and
Americans in it, had the effect of softening the focus,

changing the tone of the lighting, giving us a sense of a decent, reasonable, amiable place which, in spite of its occasional convulsions into madness and violence, was worthy of respect rather than condescension. That was the Cooke contribution. It lives on because it sowed a seed of sympathy in a generation of British people for whom there was little else to attract them to the New World.

Among his earliest broadcasts, there was one in particular that brought to British attention the potential for American politics to be a touch more interesting, a touch more vivid, than ours. On November 5th, 1948, Harry S. Truman learned that he had been re-elected in an upset that still counts as the most shocking in all American presidential history – in the words of as H. L. Menken: "a result that shook the bones of all the smarties." The Republican challenger, Thomas Dewey, is now chiefly remembered for the appearance of his name in the iconic photograph – you can still buy it today – of Truman holding up a *Chicago Tribune* newspaper whose headline reads: "Dewey Defeats Truman". The headline writers were not alone in their hubris. The *Manchester Guardian* correspondent, one Alistair Cooke, had recently sent a dispatch entitled "Harry S. Truman: A Study in Failure". The failure was not, it turned out, Truman's, but instead belonged to an entire political class – a class that had united as never before around what appeared to them to be the scientific fact that Dewey would win, a fact invented by the newly prominent polling organisations and confirmed by all right-thinking people.

Dewey was young – 46, the same age as Barack Obama when he stood for office – and he was clever and successful; a figure not dissimilar to Rudy Giuliani, the Mayor of New York who shot to fame on 9/11. Dewey was based at first in New York, fighting crime and getting the people's business done, but rose fast to national prominence. His campaign was modern – on his train there was a laundry and a public address system. You could get coffee 24 hours a day. And – the epitome of modernity – Dewey was the first presidential candidate in history to employ his own polling staff. Nothing was left to chance. That was the Dewey staff boast. And yet – as the mournful post-mortems pointed out – commentators who had trusted their guts might have been less sure of the result. There was a famous incident during the campaign when Dewey's train lurched backwards while he was speaking at Beaucoup, Illinois – the candidate was heard to mutter into the microphone that the driver ought to be shot at sunrise. As Truman's biographer David McCullough explained, "the cold arrogance of the remark did Dewey much damage". He was already known to be charmless – photographers calling out "Smile, Mr Dewey", were told, "I am." Someone wrote that he came on stage like a man mounted on castors and given a tremendous push.

By the way, Dewey also had the services of the FBI – whose boss, J. Edgar Hoover was supplying him secretly with information on his opponent. We sometimes make the mistake of thinking that the brutal, semi-legal or illegal side of American politics -- the side exemplified in recent years by Bush's brain, Karl Rove, by the politics of Chicago, by the amount of money American politics costs and the lack of clarity over what is being bought and by whom – is all something recent; that in the olden days when Dewey and Truman walked the stage, it was all rather more gentlemanly and decent. It wasn't. Not behind the scenes and not in front either – at one stage in the campaign, Truman suggested that Dewey might introduce fascism to the United States. Anyway, Truman wowed the crowds, but nothing was picked up in the polls; polls which continued to suggest an easy Dewey victory and a Republican clean sweep in the House of Representatives and in the Senate. It reminds me of the horrible night in New Hampshire during the 2008 campaign, when "all the smarties", myself included, predicted – based on the polls – that

Hillary Clinton was finished. She won, of course, and relaunched her campaign based on that victory. I like to think that Alistair Cooke would have enjoyed her achievement as much as he plainly enjoyed Truman's – once he had got over the shock. Cooke admitted his mistake and turned his broadcast into a warning against pre-judging events, a celebration of American democracy and the right of the people to change their minds and take no notice of commentators that rings down the ages. Post-war America was to have a commentator on hand to reveal to the British that the New World was fascinating and unpredictable and had fire in its belly.

And as America changed, so Alistair himself changed: a fact that made the entire enterprise all the more rewarding. He begins as a relative newcomer, but as time goes on and the layers of experience and knowledge accumulate, the result grows richer and denser. He wrote a wonderful "Letter" in 1966 about a man called Meyer Sugarman, who had written to the White House to complain because the President's party had commandeered the motel where he was intending to spend his honeymoon. The complaint secured an apology from Lyndon Johnson and the restoration of Mr and Mrs Sugarman's honeymoon plans. Alistair did not approve. He didn't say so, of course, not in so many words, but what he did say about rights and responsibilities and the stressing of the former over the latter summed up elegantly and adroitly the unspoken fears of a whole generation of Americans who viewed the 1960s with alarm.

By then the writer of *Letter from America* was, in a sense, part of that generation, able to express its forebodings with genuine feeling. Later in his career he was completely open about "where he was coming from"; he never pretended to be modern and hip and entirely comfortable with all of America's many changes of mood and tempo and direction. "I and my generation," he wrote late in life, "are probably more at home with WASPs (and a Catholic friend or two) than with the polyglot, white – black – Latino – brown – Asian, multicultural society that America has increasingly become." Commenting on the sartorial values of the newly elected Bill Clinton after the defeat of Bush senior in 1992, Alistair wrote, with gorgeous mock solemnity: "Along with the passing of George Bush we shall see, I fear, the passing of the blue blazer."

The passing of the blue blazer was also the passing of a particular facet of the relationship between Britain and America. We have, of course, lost our own blue blazers, replaced by Tony Blair's "ball-crushingly tight jeans" (as the British Ambassador Sir Christopher

Meyer referred to them), but in losing them we have not found anything to replace them in a way that brings America and Britain together. It is a generational thing and it is – as Alistair openly acknowledged – a racial thing too. He noted in that key broadcast on Bush and Clinton that the end of the blazer was the end of the old WASP-dominated America. The WASPs were our people. They were our people without really having to think about it. In fact, they were our people without thinking about it and without even knowing it. Even those Americans who despised aspects of the British – those who toyed with war with Britain over Venezuela at the end of the nineteenth century – even those people were at a deep level of subconscious being, hewn from the rock of Britain, or at least Europe.

In modern America, these blue-blazered characters are fading fast. The blue blazer is still around – John McCain fought for it valiantly as the elderly Republican presidential candidate in 2008 – but it is out of power in a big way, perhaps for ever. Obama's America is consummately unstuffy and unsteeped in the traditions and practices of the past. What would Alistair Cooke have made of it? Well, he would have loved these American times because he loved events and stories and new ways to illustrate the wonders of the New World. I suspect that he would have had great sympathy for McCain, a man of his generation and his outlook, but that he would have respected and celebrated the genius of the Obama campaign and the universally acknowledged accomplishment (for America as well as for Obama as an individual) of a black man achieving the highest office, when only a few decades earlier such a prospect looked so manifestly unrealistic. If he were writing about the election of Obama, I imagine the Cooke gaze might have been focused on the White House itself, or more precisely, on the effect on the nation of having a black family reside there.

He loved the White House, and his portraits of the contrasts between the seat of American presidential power and the British equivalents are still highly relevant. The White House had, he said, "elegance and stylish comfort" which he compared to the luxurious exile of some elderly former monarch. But he liked its American homeliness as well and did not approve of efforts to turn it into a real royal palace. He wrote hilariously about Richard Nixon's intoxication with the place: "Mr Nixon actually created a sort of palace guard. He had for ceremonial occasions a row of trumpeters in uniform." Absurd, is the Cooke view. Still, he likes us to be impressed with the place. At a dinner there with the son of a British prime minister (he was writing long after the event and we are not told who this was), he reveals that the son ruefully exclaimed, after passing through rooms blazing with glitter and glass: "Home was never like this!"

That is America and Britain. The Americans glitzy, yet in spite of their glitz, really rather uncomfortable with overt luxury – Alistair's "stylish comfort" exactly captures the White House. It is clean and warm and decked out (at least when I have been there for Christmas parties) as slightly nouveau-riche middle-class Brits might deck out their place – the Christmas tree just a little overladen and the dishes slightly too polished to be posh in a faded, furniture-inherited, British sense. But it's comfort, not grandeur, that the Americans value.

That is not to say that Alistair Cooke wrote only about himself and his own impressions of the journeys he took and the dinners he ate. He was always fascinated – in a proper journalistic fashion – by other people's stories and lives. He let them live and breathe, these actors in the American saga, and the result is that *Letter from America* simply bursts with what journalists lazily call "colour", but which is actually real life. What this enabled him to do was avoid the classic error of reporting on America as a single entity: an error that leads to the conclusion that this is a nation of gun lovers, or consumerists, or just fat people. The founding fathers referred to it as "these United States" in the plural, and now that well over 300 million people live there, the explosion of American stories and experiences is even more colossal than it was in Cooke's day. And even in his day it was quite a business, gathering intelligence on this vast nation. As a newspaperman for some of the time he wrote his "Letters" (he was the chief correspondent of the *Manchester Guardian*), Cooke was no slouch when it came to bringing in the news. He was a pioneer of the now commonplace idea that reporting America from Washington, or primarily from Washington, was a dreadful mistake. I am not entirely sure that his chosen home – Manhattan – is any more *l'Amérique profonde* than was DC, but he claimed it was easier to travel from there to other parts, and certainly being away from the federal capital, with its obsession with political minutiae, was a wonderfully liberating influence on his writing. It is vital that modern-day efforts to tell the American story to Britain and the British follow the Cooke example; we have to have folk in Washington, of course, but to report America from Washington is the equivalent of reporting China from Beijing. There is so much more. And so much that is so different.

The other lesson that can be learned from Alistair Cooke is that when British news organisations send people to America, they need to send not just their ablest political reporters but people who are genuinely open to the culture of the place. America is best reported by people who have the kind of enthusiasm for life that the United States has, or used to have. Alistair Cooke had been thought by some of his Cambridge contemporaries to be a new Noël Coward in the making. When he was sent to interview Charlie Chaplin, the two got on so well that Chaplin tried to persuade Cooke to give up journalism and collaborate with him in Hollywood. But the young reporter said no, and not because journalism was his chosen career, but because he fancied himself as a serious playwright. Alistair Cooke fizzed with ambition and drive and his interests were cultural as well as political: no wonder he devoted his life to America's big stage. He suited America as much as it turned out to suit him. We need more of these people crossing the Atlantic – fewer dull-witted cynics who want to spend their time chasing Evangelical Christians and more genuine renaissance men and women who see in America the possibilities and frailties that all humans have.

Chapter Twelve

THERE IS ANOTHER side to us and them. It has little to do with the broader questions of politics or society. It is smaller in scale than the rise of China or the size of the public debt or the future of education or the issue of gun control. It is removed from speeches made in Congress or the House of Commons. It is never on the front pages of the newspapers.

It is the internal psychological make-up of us and them; the lives not of the intellect but of the mind; the connections we make with our families and with ourselves. In the old days it would have been shrinks versus cold showers; stiff upper lips versus letting it all hang out. It is the cultural divide between us and them at the elemental level – the foundation level – of psychology.

I know something about this because I have myself lived what Americans consider to be the ultimate repressed English life. First, I went to boarding school, which only the weirdest Americans do. Secondly, I had a secret that most Americans could not in this day and age imagine keeping to themselves.

On the January 17th, 2010, at 4pm on a dull news day, the following piece was flashed by the Press Association newspaper to its subscribers around the nation:

Embargoed to 0001 Tuesday January 18
14.32 – PA – BBC PRESENTER 'SECRET SON OF NEWSREADER'
By Anthony Barnes, Press Association

Radio 4 presenter Justin Webb has revealed for the first time he is the secret son of respected newsreader Peter Woods.

The Today programme host, 50, had no contact with his late father apart from a brief encounter at the age of six months and has kept his identity under wraps throughout his life.

Woods was a celebrated host of the BBC's flagship Nine O'Clock News and one of the great characters of his day. Famously, one BBC2 bulletin in the 1970s had to be faded out when he was audibly slurring his words. Webb has gone public about his father by writing about him for the first time in the new edition of Radio Times. Webb said he "buried" his father's identity in his mind to the extent he felt little connection and never considered getting in touch, even when he followed in the same career.

I was 50: just a few days past my birthday. From the moment I first knew – when I suppose I was five or six – to that day, I had told only my wife and (I think I remember rightly) one very discreet friend at university. My mother had told my parents-in-law, and her sister and brother also knew. That was it. A secret about the most fundamental facts of where I came from – who my father was – had been kept throughout my childhood and most of my adult life. Americans have secrets too but not, generally, of this kind. Americans share. With friends and – if they are relatively wealthy – with an entire industry of professional listeners. America is a nation devoted to what the medical folk call "talking therapies". It is, more than any other nation on earth, the home of exploration of the self.

Are we going in their direction in Britain? And if so, at what cost, and with what benefits?

A late-autumn day on the beach at Seaton in South Devon. It is desolate in a way that only the English seaside can manage. Gloomy overweight families, unaccountably late in their holidaymaking (waiting for the really cheap rates, perhaps?) sit vacant-eyed in fish and chip shops. The wind is cold and the pebble-dashed houses huddle back from the beach. People are boarding up, winterising. There is still icecream but only the hardiest have the stomach for it.

On the beach – behind a slightly torn wind barrier – sit two figures. A mother and a son have made a nest among the pebbles. She's not yet old – perhaps in her forties – and he looks about ten or twelve. Why, when I see them, do I have the urge to stare? To walk up to them, to hug them both and tell them: "It can be ok! This life – this intense love and this gaping hole where a father should be – it can eventually give way to normality and a life happily lived."

We are visiting a relative and we have an hour to kill. To amuse my own children – who have not noticed the only other people on the beach – I go into the water. I have always enjoyed the shock of swimming in extreme cold – one day it may kill me but there are worse ways to go. My wife Sarah and our children laugh and toy with coming in themselves, then give up on the idea but from the windbreak twenty yards away I notice a movement. The boy and his mother are coming down to the water's edge and the boy is ready to pull off his sweatshirt and come in himself. It is cold – very cold – but he is powered by something I recognise instantly as unstoppable. He wants to test himself against the elements and to do so in the presence of another man. He wants to get away from the comforting but cloying closeness with Mum and have a go at something painful – something from which a mother, any mother, would instinctively withdraw, but into which a father, any father, would plunge recklessly, knowing that half the fun of being male is contained in foolish plunges into all kinds of trouble.

For a few minutes we swim about, he and I. We exchange only a few words – he is not there to talk. We are buffeted by freezing waves; hit hard and smashed onto the stones. Eventually, worried I might actually have a heart attack and spoil the whole day, I get out and salute him. He waves. He looks radiantly, gloriously happy. And as I turn away I feel like crying.

Of course, I have no way of knowing whether they really were a mother and son with no father. Perhaps Dad was at home or at work. I could have misunderstood the whole thing. But I doubt it: I have antennae for these things. I am not the world's brightest, most emotionally intelligent being (my wife says) but I know a mother and son alone when I see them. I know them because I was in that team. I spent a whole childhood sitting on the beach hoping for a man to come along and take me for a dangerous swim. A whole childhood looking after Mum, loving Mum, but unsure about how this would end.

Incompleteness is a secret many British people keep. Sad, lonely childhoods are not, it is fair to say, entirely unusual. Plenty of successful people feel themselves driven through their lives by a sense of loss experienced while young, or simply by the spur of trying to escape from circumstances that were in some way desperate; a lack of love, or poverty, perhaps. Our early lives, thank goodness, do not shape us in ways that cannot be reordered later, and, sometimes, we manage to find ways of taking charge and using adversity to build firmer foundations for the future. We do it as adults but we often do it, almost unconsciously, as children.

Here is where it gets complicated in my case and in the cases of dozens of people who have written to me since I revealed that my father was Peter Woods. I grew up with a sense of longing and a sense of loss – actually there was a man in the house, Charles, whom my mother married when I was three or four, but he was mentally ill and cold and distant. He was never Dad. (My mother used to tell the story of how, when I was young, I asked her one day: "Where did we *get* Charles?") But this oddness was compounded by another.

I was always aware that there was something I knew about my life and could never reveal to others; something my mother had not exactly banned but talked of only with reluctance.

What I have found revealing about the kind notes and emails I received after I spoke out about my father, was quite how many told of similar secrets and the effects those secrets can have. Being brought up by Mum is generally looked back on – perhaps particularly by boys – as perfectly survivable. In fact, I think I read somewhere that the concentration of affection it entails can be regarded as a good thing – strong women can bring up strong men: Barack Obama is a shining example. But the secretiveness is less easy to chalk up as a potential plus.

Did you know your father? Well, no is the answer I used to give to acquaintances who enquired, I did not know him because he had left. Did you know anything about him: did you have any contact with him? That was trickier; do you have *contact* with someone if you watch them on the TV every night? I suppose you could argue that this is not contact as generally understood, but you begin to feel like Bill Clinton disputing – during the Monica Lewinsky affair – the meaning of the word "is". With this answer – I had no contact with him – I was in the realms of revealing so much less than the full truth that it was becoming a lie.

A necessary lie? What would have happened if I had popped up on Peter Woods's doorstep when I was in my twenties? It would have shocked and upset his wife and family and distressed my mother. It would have linked me publicly to him rather than let me make my own way in journalism. It would have been a big story at a bad moment.

So I never did it. And when, during the first Gulf War, I sat by an Egyptian army tank waiting to drive into Kuwait, and a cameraman told me about some trip he had done with Peter Woods and the fun they had had, I just kept quiet. On many other occasions too, when he was mentioned I said nothing. Like a character in a spy novel, I compartmentalised my life. And that compartment was closed and locked and buried.

And here is the point: I think it was the right thing to do. Many of the people who have been in touch with me since I wrote my piece have talked about the relief they felt when a similar secret could finally be shared. But many too have made it clear that there was a right moment for that secret to be shared, and that sometimes we have to accept that that moment might not come at all, not even on our death-beds. No man is an island. We have a responsibility one to another which transcends the "need to know" or the need to be honest and open. We live in a Wikileaks age where transparency is celebrated by some as an end in itself. This, I think, is wrong. My secret was painful and probably damaging if I am to be brutally honest: it reduced me as a person. But the keeping of it also made me. It kept the relationship with my mother loving and fulfilling for her and me until the day she died. It protected Peter Woods and his family.

It could never have happened in America. There are two conversations that Americans are willing to have that very few Brits could or would want to match. The first is what the pastor said in church last Sunday. Seriously, people talk about their pastors. It's like Ambridge. But the second and even stranger is the conversation that begins with the words: "I was telling my analyst exactly that last Tuesday…"

From an early age, Americans are taught that to have a mental life that is not on show to someone else is a mistake. The conditioning is subtle at first but very soon becomes highly significant. "How does this make you feel?" is a question my children, growing up in America, had to get used to being asked even if their atavistic Britishness made them regard it as otiose. "Johnny hit you? And how does that make you feel?" The questions invite sarcasm, another British vice, but also invite children to explore those feelings that, frankly, they feel they should have even if they haven't. It is, in other words, an invitation to false memory syndrome. The author Gertrude Stein, returning to California and wanting to visit her childhood home, couldn't find it and declared: "There was no there there." Mentally, in America, if there is no there there, you invent a there. And you make it sound as you expect the adults will want it to sound. You embellish. You imagine. It is gloriously unhealthy and makes for some pretty messed-up children. To be frank about our children's friends at school, there were quite a few whose exploration of their inner selves was deeply damaging as well as deeply boring. I can remember one girl asking my wife Sarah: "Do you like me?" The girl was eight. It was, to use an American expression, inappropriate. Why would an eight-year-old wonder about such a thing? American culture has encouraged too much self-analysis.

Then comes adulthood and the show goes on. Several friends of ours had professional help with their innermost thoughts. Weekly sessions would explore who said what to whom when they were fourteen. Did the move to New Mexico really hurt more than it seemed at the time? Was Dad's new job never properly explained to you? This narcissism was epitomised in a book about working mothers called *Mommy Wars*, written by a friend of ours. In it she delved, in excruciating detail, into her thoughts about her husband. The poor man has inscribed our copy thus: "Don't believe everything you read about me!" Jesus, it hardly mattered whether we did or not. The ghastly intimacy – the assumption that psychological details about your life and your unwilling partner's life are somehow better aired than not aired – is an American disaster story. It leads to an inability to cope with adversity – there is always something, someone, to blame – and it can waste huge amounts of time that would be better spent in other pursuits.

I suppose they would say that the silent approach I adopted towards my strange upbringing must have brought all sorts of hang-ups and weirdness with it, and who am I to deny it? Any sensible analysis of them and us has to acknowledge that in every area there are aspects of American behaviour that seem superior and aspects of British behaviour that come out on top. In this particular area I think we win: the stiff upper lip has some benefits for society generally, especially when times are tough. If the answer to the question "Who is to blame?" turns out to be "me", there is sanity to be retrieved in this uncomfortable fact. One of the big issues America faces in the coming years is whether it can avoid going to the shrink so often.

I resist the temptation to end with a grand conclusion about the bigger relationship between them and us. We are very different and would benefit, I think, from noting those differences more clearly. We are linked because we think we are linked but that link may be called into question and disregarded in the future. We need to be free of them and they need to be free of us. We are also – on each side of the Atlantic – facing deep fissures within our own societies. America is bold and beautiful but flawed and tawdry; Britain is steely and elegant but sometimes seems drunken and self-deluding. Having spent the best years of my professional life in America, I hold the place in the highest regard. My youngest child is a US citizen and when she becomes president I hope she has the rest of us to stay and salutes her special relationship with us. But she lives at a time when the wider special relationship has become a hindrance to clear thinking and ultimately to the continuance of the values of the English-speaking world. We need a divorce so that our children can prosper, free of the bickering and the plate-throwing and the stale emptiness and the pretence. We need two homes and an amicable division of the furniture. We could even marry other people one day and, as with the best divorces, all be friends.

Chapter Thirteen

OWEN BENNETT JONES is one of the BBC's finest and most diligent journalists. Gangly and academic-looking, sporting formal shirts but without cuff links, topped off by a punch-up of a hairdo – thick, white and apparently fired up by electrical charges in the manner of Albert Einstein – he is the last man you would want to visit you as you enjoyed the fruits of retirement after a long period as the leader of a one party state. Owen is a persistent questioner, a difficult man to throw off the scent.

But this is the fate that befell Todor Zhivkov, who is remembered now, if at all, as the boss of Bulgaria when Bulgaria was an outpost of the Soviet empire. He was, to put it mildly, a bit of a toady, even by the standards of the times. Originally a fan of Stalin, he managed to ally himself more or less gracefully with those who denounced Stalin and, over a long period as head of the Bulgarian state, he moved with speed to keep the nation on the right footing with Moscow. When

Moscow seemed to be toying with private markets, he toyed with them too; when they pulled back, he pulled back. When Moscow broke with the Chinese, he broke with the Chinese. Zhivkov was up for the Cold War fight; he ran a much-feared secret police service and networks of informers operated throughout Bulgarian society. He used prison camps to incarcerate his opponents. He built motorways with no central reservations so that Soviet warplanes could land on them in the event of a war with the West. When the playwright Georgi Markov rejected efforts by the regime to co-opt him into Bulgarian state-ordered life and went to live in London, Zhivkov, it is widely believed, was the man who ordered Markov killed. Famously, it happened as Markov was on his way to the BBC World Service building in Aldwych in central London, when an assassin pricked him with a poison-tipped umbrella.

Zhivkov valued loyalty. Throughout his time in power, he surrounded himself with those who exhibited *predanost* (keen devotion, unquestioning allegiance) and woe betide those who failed to be entirely convincing, and those who opted, dangerously, for outright opposition.

Bennett Jones had come to try to discover the truth of one of the oddest episodes of Bulgarian communist history – an episode potentially even more troubling to

Zhivkov than the Markov affair. And here is the question on Owen's lips as he finally gained access to the
former leader of Bulgaria in his retirement home in the
capital, Sofia. After some pleasantries and chat about
the modern world, he asked Zhivkov bluntly: was it
true or was it not true that his loyalty to the Soviet
Union resulted, on at least one occasion, in Zhivkov
actually offering to abandon Bulgaria's existence as a
separate state – an act of unique self un-determination
even in the world behind the Iron Curtain, and opt
instead to become a province – a province mind, not a
separate country – state or county of Soviet Russia?

You will not be surprised to learn that Owen left the
retirement home not much the wiser. Zhivkov did not
entirely deny the charge but did not entirely accept it
either. Now he is dead.

Bulgaria was an extreme case. But you could argue,
with a touch of hyperbole perhaps, that the same choices
open to Zhivkov and the same motivations have been
present for every British prime minister since Suez saw
the end of real British power: to fold into the American
empire or to hold back. This question haunted them
and haunts them still, at least in shadowy form. Some
held back – Wilson during Vietnam is a good example
– and some took the Zhivkov approach. Would Tony
Blair have turned down a full Washington–London

merger if he had got to be the figurehead? Who knows?

The Blair years came to an end with Britain still an independent nation – a fact perhaps doubted by some at the height of his friendship with George W. Bush. It might even be the case that the wobbles about independence during the Blair years have led to a firmer sense now of the need for Britain to assert itself. We are able finally to say our goodbyes and go our own ways; to continue to benefit from this relationship but to benefit as well from the joy of independence. We can celebrate our differences today as cordially as we have, over the years, celebrated our similarities.

Perhaps the constitutional chasm between us and them would always have prevented proper union. I have made the point in this book that we treat executive power very differently – the British embrace it with the fervour of subjects, the Americans distrust it with the zealousness of revolutionaries. The fate that befell President Bush was an example of the oddness of a political system in which presidents are battling constantly and often in vain against a set-up that deals much of the power to others. A colleague of mine went to interview Bush. It was towards the end of his time in office and to a large extent the White House had given up the ghost. They were going through the motions.

But for the BBC, any interview with any president is a big deal, so my colleague did his best and filled the twentieth minutes with trenchant questions on a wide range of issues. At the end, the President offered to sign pieces of paper for my colleague's children. And he went further: how about a quick tour? Wonderful, thought my colleague, and followed the President to the library and then to the Rose Garden. It was all superbly relaxed and amiable. But as the President proposed the next part of the tour – to the Oval Office itself – the BBC man began to worry. This interview was being keenly awaited by several BBC programmes. They would be wondering where he was. They would be filling spaces in their schedules with increasing desperation. So he heard himself say, to the President of the United States of America: "Umm, Mr President, I don't want to appear rude, but I really must be going as I have, umm, things to do..."

No British prime minister is ever quite so much at a loose end. And if the constitutional separateness does not convince you, how about the psychological separateness? Again, George W. Bush provides an example. Years ago my friend, the *Times* reporter Tim Reid, was meeting President Bush at what they call a grip-and-grin session in the White House. It was Christmas and Tim's wife Helena also came along. The amount of time you have with the great personage at these sessions is limited with even greater strictness than at a Royal event. Secret service men usher you in, an announcement is made about who you are, you smile and grip and grin, a photo is taken, and you go. There is little time for small-talk.

Tim and Helena were ushered in and announced – "Mr and Mrs Tim Reid from *The Times* of England!"

President Bush, friendly and keen to please as he always was in these one-to-one events, apparently remembered that he had recently been interviewed by *The Times* of England, but here his memory understandably failed him. The interview had actually been carried out by the editor who had, by this time, hopped on a plane back to London, so when the President presented his hand to Tim and said, "Howdy Tim, I think we met recently?", poor Tim was faced, as a quintessentially English Englishman, with a ticklish problem. How to let the President down gently? How to avoid the rudeness of a denial of their meeting but at the same time avoid going along with an untruth?

As Tim tells it, after a pause that seemed to him to be excrutiatingly long, he came up with a form of words that was both completely English and also completely barmy: "Ah, Mr President, umm, I am not sure that we actually did!"

Bush – nonplussed – turned to Helena and whispered: "You'd have thought he'd have remembered!"

How foolish we can sometimes seem to our cousins! Poor President Bush, reviled and harassed by a thousand British commentators, tries his best to be polite to a Brit he meets in the flesh and that's the thanks he gets. Truly, we are separated by so much more than our common language.

America is a foreign country. This is a fact that bears repeating. It bears keeping in mind during all our dealings with them and theirs with us. The relationship that develops from this awareness could be so much healthier. We can genuinely celebrate our joint refusal, for instance, to give up on a commitment to democracy and open societies. We can bicker cheerfully about language and sexual mores and even religion: their religiosity and our pagan wantonness. We can learn from America's zest for life and belief that the world can be shaped and bettered. They can learn from our moderation and our maturity. But what we must not do is confuse ourselves with them – we should not let affection turn into longing and then into frustration when they continue to own guns and drive large cars. We have to let go. In 2020, we will celebrate the

400th anniversary of the *Mayflower* sailing. Already commemorative events are being planned on both sides of the Atlantic. How about an extra one? An affectionate burning of a (specially created) Grand Seal of the Special/Essential Relationship – finally, a true declaration of mutual independence.

Acknowledgements

I would like to thank the hundreds of people – public figures and private individuals – who contributed to the ideas in this book. To single out just a few: Adrian and Amelia Wooldridge, David and Genia Chavchevadze, David Frum, Sir Nigel and Lady Sheinwald, Lord and Lady McNally, Ben Preston and Janice Turner, Simon and Ulrike Wilson, Mark Damazer, Ceri Thomas, and Adi Raval, without whose Herculean efforts I would not have met and interviewed Barack Obama. I am grateful to the staff of the British Library of Political and Economic Science at the London School of Economics for their assistance with historical documents and to the Foreign Affairs Committee of the House of Commons for inviting me to speak to them about the special relationship. None of these institutions or individuals is, of course, the slightest bit responsible for anything I have got wrong. Nor is my wife, Sarah, though I should finish by thanking her for her love and support and critical reading of everything I write.

Justin Webb was named political journalist of the year for his reporting on America during Barack Obama's rise to power. He spent eight years in Washington for the BBC and one of his children is a US citizen. He is now a presenter of the *Today* programme on Radio Four.